THE SECRET SOCIETIES

OF ALL AGES AND COUNTRIES

VOLUME II

THE SECRET SOCIETIES

OF ALL AGES AND COUNTRIES

VOLUME II

BY

CHARLES WILLIAM HECKETHORN

Athens ‡ Manchester

The Secret Societies of all Ages and Countries

Volume II

Old Book Publishing Ltd

Book Cover Design: Old Book Publishing Ltd

Title of original: The Secret Societies of all Ages and Countries.Volume II

Originally published in 1875

Cover Image: Ismail lion calligram symbolising the lion of God.

ISBN–10: 1-78107-200-0 volume I
ISBN–10: 1-78107-201-9 **volume II**
ISBN–10: 1-78107-202-7 set

ISBN–13: 978-1-78107-200-4 volume I
ISBN–13: 978-1-78107-201-1 **volume II**
ISBN–13: 978-1-78107-202-8 set

Editor's Note

THE SECRET SOCIETIES

OF ALL AGES AND

COUNTRIES.

BY

CHARLES WILLIAM HECKETHORN.

IN TWO VOLUMES.

VOL. II.

FIDE ET FIDUCIA

LONDON:

RICHARD BENTLEY AND SON,

Publishers in Ordinary to Her Majesty,

NEW BURLINGTON STREET.

1875.

ANALYTICAL TABLE OF CONTENTS.

The numbers refer to the §.

VOLUME II.

Book IX.

MYSTICS.

Book XIII.

CARBONARI.

Book XIV.

THE INQUISITION.

Book XV.

MINOR ITALIAN SECTS.

Book XVI.

YOUTH.

BOOK XVII.

MISCELLANEOUS SOCIETIES.

CORRECTIONS AND ADDITIONS.

VOL. I.

Page 8, line 5 from bottom, for " appositions" read " apparitions."

P. 31, l. 8 from top, for " How" read " Now."

P. 31, l. 9 from top, for " How" read " Now."

P. 31, l. 9 from bottom, for " Ihot" read " Thot."

P. 54, l. 11 from top, after " Legend of the Temple," insert " (191)."

P. 61, l. 2 from top, for " Iabulon" read " Jabulon."

P. 78, l. 5 from top. Cadmus is not to be understood to signify a man. The Phenician word " cadm" means " the East," hence the meaning of the passage is, that the mysteries and learning came from that quarter.

P. 90, l. 12 from bottom, for " from" read " with."

P. 97, l. 2 from top, after " hereafter" insert " (78)."

P. 117, l. 1 from top, for " shameful" read " changeful."

P. 118. To list of authorities, add, " Molitor's Philosophie der Geschichte."

P. 139, last line. " Cathari" means the " pure."

P. 149, l. 3 from top, " *Langue d'Oïl*," more correctly " *Langue d'Ouï.*"

P. 150, l. 3 from bottom, after (*which see*) place (272-277).

P. 158. A green glass vase, said to be the original San Graal, is preserved in the cathedral of Genoa, and considered so valuable that it requires a special permission from the municipality to see it.

P. 194, § 163. To the derivation of the term " Baphomet" suggested in the text, may be added that from the Provencal *bafa*, a falsehood.

P. 196, l. 9 from top, for " Moulay" read " Molay."

P. 204, l. 10 from top, for " him" read " them."

P. 227, l. 6 from top, for " X " read " + "

P. 238. To list of Masonic authorities, add, " *Origine de la Maçonnerie Adonhiramite.* Helyopolis, 1787."

P. 259, l. 6 from top, after " ⟁ " insert " or ⊔."

P. 280, l. 1 from bottom, for " 210 " read " 212."

P. 290, l. 4 from bottom, for " Jebunah" read " Tehunah."

P. 331, l. 4 from bottom, between "masons" and "turned" insert "it is averred."

P. 345, l. 3 from bottom, for "Abatement" read "Abasement."

P. 358, l. 3 from bottom, for "*passer*" read "*fourrer*."

P. 384. Add at end of chapter, "According to the *Almanacco del Libero Muratore* for 1873, there are now in existence 89 Grand Lodges and 11,678 Lodges, with rather more than two millions of members.

VOL. II.

P. 10, l. 11 from bottom, for "explanation." read "explanation—"

P. 10, l. 8 from bottom, for "Sophia, heavenly Virgin," read "The heav'nly Virgin Sophia."

P. 10, l. 3 from bottom, for "abysmal" read "abyssal."

P. 11, l. 1 from top, for "No" read "Its."

P. 11, l. 8 from top, for "in" read "is."

P. 11, l. 12 from top, for "thought" read "Nought."

P. 11, l. 13 from top, for "bent on self-manifesting" read "in self-manifestation."

P. 11, l. 3 from bottom, for "Whilom the wise Sophia showed" read "was whilom shown by Sophia to."

P. 12, l. 6 from top, for "Sophia, Virgin," read "The Virgin Sophia" (Sóphïa, in theosophy, is pronounced as shown, with classical accentuation on the first syllable, the *i* being short).

P. 14, l. 3 from bottom, for "Leadley" read "Lead."

P. 82, l. 9 from bottom, for "fitches" read "finches."

BOOK IX.

MYSTICS.

"*Chorus Mysticus.*

"Alles Vergängliche
Ist nur ein Gleichniss;
Das Unzulängliche
Hier wird's Ereigniss;
Das Unbeschreibliche
Hier ist's gethan;
Das Ewig-Weibliche
Zieht uns hinan."—*Faust.*

"The wisest of the pagan world, and their greatest philosophers, held Theurgic Magic in the highest esteem. Theurgy was, according to them, a divine art which served only to advance the mind of man to the highest perfection, and they who by means of this magic had the happiness to arrive at what they called *Autopsia* or *Intuition*, a state wherein they enjoyed intimate intercourse with the gods, believed themselves invested with all their power."—MAYO.

"It was anciently believed in all nations that there were means whereby men and women might come to have some acquaintance and communication with God."—*An Introduction to Theosophy.*

AUTHORITIES.

Matter. Saint-Martin, le Philosophe inconnn, sa Vie, et ses Ecrits, son Maître Martinez et leurs Groupes. Paris, 1862.

Swedenborg. Works *passim.*

Matter. Emmanuel de Swedenborg : sa Vie, ses Ecrits et sa Doctrine. Paris, 1863.

Böhme. Works *passim.*

Gérard de Nerval. Les Illuminés. Paris, 1852.

I.

JACOB BÖHME.

296.

PARALLEL *between Mystics and Sectaries.*—All secret societies have some connection with mysticism, secret itself, delighting in mystery, as the loving soul delights in surrounding the beloved object with mystery. Sectaries to some extent are the parents of mystics. The silent adoration of the Infinite, in which mystics delight, has its counterpart in the worship of progress, liberty, and truth, to which sectaries devote themselves. Progress, liberty, truth, are attributes of the Divine; whoso loves these attributes, loves and apprehends God. The mystics are the men of thought, the sectaries the men of action. However remote the thoughts of the former may seem from application to everyday life, from political strife, they yet have a positive influence on human belief and will. The

mystics behold in paradise that same ideal, trans-
figured, enlarged, and perpetuated, which the sectaries pursue on earth.

297. *Character and Mission of Mystics.*—The
mystics · continue the school of ancient initiations,
which to many nations were their only philosophy,
science, and liberty. They are the priests of In-
finity; in their tenderness they are the most tole-
rant of men, pardoning all, even the devil; they
embrace all, pity all. They are, in a certain sense,
the rationalists of prayer. By means of syntheses,
trances, and raptures, they arrive at a pure and
simple understanding of the supernatural, which
they adore more with their imagination and affection, than with the learned and sophisticated con-
ceits of theology. Therefore the mystics of all
creeds resemble each other; theirs is a region common to all religions, the universal home of the soul
—a height from which the innumerable horizons of
conscience are seen to meet.

298. *Merits of Böhme.*—The prince of mystics
is without contradiction Jacob Böhme; in fact,
compared with him, all other mystics sink into utter
insignificance, as *mere* visionaries, whose rhapso-
dies, though sometimes poetical, were always fan-
tastical and useless to the world, because not
founded on the truths of Eternal Nature. Böhme
was a visionary, but a visionary of the stamp of
Columbus; to him also it was given to behold with

his mental eye a hidden world, the world of the Properties of Eternal Nature, and to solve the great mystery, not of this earth alone, but of the universe. He was emphatically a *central* philosopher, who from his standpoint could survey the whole sphere, within and without, and not merely an outer segment of its shell. He could therefore see the *causes* of things, and not their effects only. There is, I do not deny it, much in the writings of Böhme that cannot be maintained or proved, much that appears as pure alchymistical and cabalistic reverie, the disease of the age in which he lived. But though he may often be wrong in his deductions, he is always right in fundamentals. And even after rejecting all that is doubtful or absolutely erroneous, there is left so much which science and experiment demonstrate to be absolutely true, that it is hard to remember that all this was enunciated by a man who had no learning and never made an experiment in his life, and at a time when none of the scientific truths he put forth were even dreamt of by scientific men. Even if he had made known nothing but the Seven Properties of Nature (11), the key to all her mysteries, he would for ever rank among the greatest lights of science. I confess I am at a perfect loss to account for this extraordinary knowledge in an untutored shoemaker, such as Böhme was. If there were any work extant, or known to have been extant before or at his time, in which an account of the Seven Properties was given, I should say, he must have copied from that, though this theory would still leave the original discoverer unknown; but no trace either actual or traditional of any such work, or of the knowledge of these properties—except of such as is implied in the universal veneration in which the number seven has ever been held —is anywhere discoverable. Whence then did Böhme derive his knowledge? No one who has studied its details can doubt of their truth. No one before him has put them forth. Is then intuition possible? Was Böhme endowed with that gift? This is in fact a greater secret than any handed down in any secret society, ancient or modern. Of course scientific men, as they are called, laugh at Böhme, as a mad dreamer, just as the Royal Society laughed at the electric discoveries of Franklin—he was a printer who had actually worked at the press, what could he know of electricity? How could he solve a problem that had puzzled the most learned of their members? And how can Böhme, the despised and illiterate shoemaker, teach the scientists of our day anything? But the fact remains, that in the writings of this poor cobbler lie the germs of all the discoveries in physical science hitherto, and yet to be, made.

299. *Böhme's Influence.*—I am well aware that this assertion will again meet with the derision it has hitherto encountered. Yet the reader who

has accompanied me thus far, ought to pause, ere he joins the laughers. He will have had ample proofs that I accept nothing on mere authority, however high it may be considered. I want proof, positive proof, of any alleged fact, before I accept it as fact. If therefore with this disposition on my part, and after the study of Böhme's works, pursued for a number of years, with opportunities such as few have had—for the hierophant that initiated me into the mysteries of the German theosopher is undoubtedly the most learned Böhmite in this or any other country; in fact, the only man that understands him thoroughly—if under these circumstances I entertain the opinions expressed in the foregoing paragraph, they cannot well be without foundation. But whoso is not to be convinced by Böhme's demonstration of the Seven Properties cannot be convinced by any argument. And Böhme's writings have not been without a deep and lasting, though latent, influence on modern philosophy and science. Even Newton was largely indebted to him. Among Sir Isaac's papers there were found large extracts out of Böhme's works, written with his own hand; and he thence learnt that attraction is the first and fundamental law of nature. Of course the scientific elaboration of the axiom is all Newton's own, and it detracts nothing from his glory that he learnt the law from Böhme. Newton even went further; he and Dr.

Newton, his relative, set up furnaces, and were for
several months hard at work in quest of the tincture
so largely spoken of by Böhme. But the influence
of this author is still more strikingly seen in the
writings of Francis Baader, a German physicist of
the present day, who has pursued his scientific en-
quiries by the light—feebly caught, it is true, in
his mind's mirror—of Böhme's revelations. The
greatest philosophic thinkers of this and the preceding century have drunk at the spring of Böhme's
writings; and the systems of Leibnitz, Laplace,
Schelling, Hegel, Fichte, and others, are distinctly
permeated by his spirit—but none sufficiently, and
hence no one of their systems is satisfactory. Goethe
was well versed in Böhme, and many allusions in
his writings, which the critics can make nothing of,
may be explained by passages from Böhme. Thus
the commentators and translators of " Faust" have
made the most ridiculous guesses as to the meaning
to be attached to the "Mothers," to whom Faust
is to descend in his search for Helen. The
" Mothers " are the first three properties of nature (11), and all the instructions given by Mephistopheles to Faust before his descent *ad inferos*
is a highly poetical, and at the same time philosophical, description of them. If scientific men,
instead of laughing at Böhme, would study his
works, we should have no Darwinism, no theories
of the sun's refrigeration, and no president of the

British Association propounding the monstrous doctrine that life on this earth had its origin in the life carried hither on fragments struck off other planets and celestial bodies and falling on this globe—-a theory which, even could it for one moment be entertained, would still leave *the* question, "Whence came life?" unanswered. Nor should we have the Huxleys and Tyndalls assuming that life can be put into a creature, after its material body is made, which is no better than assuming that a circle and its roundness are two separate things—that first comes the figure and afterwards its roundness. Böhme, whom they look upon as a dreamer, would show them, the real dreamers, that life makes the body to manifest itself; when a growing acorn puts forth sprouts, it is the life creeping out, feeling its way, and clothing itself in matter as it goes along, and in order to go along. Let scientists read that magnificent chapter beginning with: "We see that all life is essential; it manifests itself by the germing of the essences." What theology might learn from Böhme, cannot be comprised in a few words: the vexed questions of the origin of evil, predestination, Christ's flesh and blood which are to regenerate man, their nature and action, are all profoundly and scientifically expounded in the writings of this author. But as he had no academic title, nor even common education, they despise him; and yet some of these very men will put faith in equally illiterate swindling spiritualists, who delude the world with the most childish and absurd nonsense. Let me close these remarks on Böhme with some lines, composed as a tribute to his excelling merits.

300. *Jacob Böhme—A Poem.—*

Emblazoned in a sheen of mystic splendour,
  Crowned with the seer's bright aureola,
The only true expounder and defender
  ·Of triune faith and every being's law ;
A scribe, inspired in mortal words to render
  What he in beatific vision saw :
Behold the solitary mental freeman,
The centrally illumined Jacob Behmen.

Yea, Jacob Behmen.   Although but a cobbler,
  With small endowment of scholastic lore,
And by the outward world believed a gobbler
  Of idle tales, his crazy fancy bore ;
Of mystic crudities a tedious babbler,
  Inventing words that make the lips right sore
Of those attempting their pronunciation,
And mad all brains that try their explanation.

To him revealed in radiance overpowering
  Were all divine and natural mysteries ;
Sophia, heavenly Virgin, on him showering
  Her choicest gifts, her boundless love and bliss,
Endowed his mental eye with vision towering
  As far beyond this earth as heaven is ;
Enabled him in ecstasy to enter
The first abysmal Nothing's hidden centre.

To search into the innermost divinity,
  The secret working of the groundless Will ;

No self-revealment as a conscious trinity,
    A triune'life, and yet one Godhead still;
The ever-generating pure Virginity,
    Whence all the essences of life distil,
And are into that magic Mirror moulded,
Through which Eternal Nature is unfolded.

To see in Maja's mirror, more ethereal
    Than in the solar light, man's subtlest thought,
Creation's first Aurora, dawn empyreal,
    By the divine Imagination wrought,
Assuming form, becoming the material
    And visible reflection of the thought,
When it, bent on self-manifesting, sunders
Its powers, virtues, colours, wonders.

To watch the festive time of nature's vernal
    And universal palingenesis,
The bridal of the properties eternal,
    When Light—the last three—with a thrilling kiss,
Doth fill the first three of the life infernal—
    The Darkness—with its all-transmuting bliss.
And in the fourth—the Fire—this bride is won,
Whose mundane nuptial chamber is the Sun.

But slow and painful is the toil of science,
    Which evermore to outward matter clings;
The Life to all research doth bid defiance,
    Unknown to schools remains the Cause of things;
But Knowledge freely, and with pleased compliance,
    Into the arms of Intuition springs.
Hence, all that science ever shall discover,
Whilom the wise Sophia showed her lover.

Her lover and her husband—for united
    To him she was by close and loving ties;

Her lustre his dark earthly being lighted—
In love man's true transfiguration lies—
His fiery soul her gentle light ignited,
And fire subdued by light is paradise;
And thus as his celestial life and leman
Sophia, Virgin, dwelt in Jacob Behmen.

301. *Sketch of Böhme's Life.*—Jacob Böhme was born at Görlitz in Upper Lusatia in 1575. In his childhood he was engaged in tending cattle. In this solitary life and the constant contemplation of nature, he felt himself a poet, and, as he imagined, destined for great things. He saw an occult meaning in all the voices of the country; and, believing that therein he heard the voice of God, he lent his ear to a revelation he regarded as coming from God Himself through the medium of nature. At the age of fifteen or sixteen he was apprenticed to a shoemaker at Görlitz. The sedentary occupation increased his tendency to mysticism. Severe and zealous for good manners and morals, and quite wrapped up in himself, he was considered proud by some, and mad by others. And indeed, having received no education whatever, his ideas were necessarily confused, obscure, and disconnected. In 1594 he married. Though a good husband and good father, he did not cease from being a visionary; and, driven to it by frequent dreams, which he attributed to the influence of the Holy Spirit, he finally decided on writing. His first

work was the " Aurora," the best known, but the most imperfect, of all his writings, both as regards style and matter. It brought upon him the persecution of the clergy, at whose instance the magistracy of Görlitz prohibited his writing any more— an order which he obeyed for a number of years ; but eventually the promptings of his spirit were no longer to be withstood, and he entirely gave himself up to the composition of his numerous writings during the last six years of his life, in which he produced among other works the " Mysterium Magnum," the " Signatura Rerum," the " Threefold Life," the " Six Theosophic Points," the " Divine Contemplation," the " Supersensual Life," all of which contain amidst much that is incongruous, whimsical, obscure, and unintelligible, passages of such profound knowledge and comprehensive meaning that no true philosopher dares to despise them, and which in fact will yet be recognised as the only solid bases of all true science. Now, and then we meet in his writings with passages of such poetic beauty, such lofty views of Deity and nature, as surpass all the conceptions of the greatest poets of all ages. His works, written in German, during his life-time circulated only in manuscript; they were afterwards translated into Dutch, and from this language they were rendered into English. The German edition of his works, full of errors, did not appear until 1682. In France, St.-Martin, *le Philosophe Inconnu,*

translated some of them into French.   His greatest
commentator was Dionysius Andreas Freher, a German who lived many years in this country, and whose
works, all written in English—with the exception
of two, written in German, and translated by the
present writer—exist only in manuscript, copies of
some of them being in the British Museum, whilst
the originals are in the possession of a private
gentleman. William Law, the learned English divine,
who had the use of these MSS., is his greatest
English commentator; his " Appeal," " Way to
Divine Knowledge," " Spirit of Prayer," and
" Spirit of Love," show how well he had seized
the leading ideas of Böhme's system.   Böhme died
in 1624, his last words being: " Now I am going
into paradise."

302. *The Philadelphians.*—Böhme himself never
founded any sect.   He was too much wrapt up in
his glorious visions to think of gathering disciples
and perpetuating his name by such means ; like the
sun, he shed his light abroad, because it was his
nature to do so, unheedful whether it fell on rich
or barren ground, leaving it to fructify according
to its own inherent qualities.   And the fruit is to
come yet.   For the society of the " Philadelphians,"
founded towards the close of the seventeenth century, by Jane Leadley, whose vain visions undoubtedly were the result of her study of the work
of Böhme, never led to any results spiritual or

scientific. The society in fact only existed about seven years, and its members had but vague and imperfect notions of the meaning and tendency of the writings of their great master.

II.

EMANUEL SWEDENBORG.

303.

EMANUEL SWEDENBORG.—A mystic, who as yet has made much more noise in the world, though totally unworthy of being compared with Jacob Böhme—for this latter has left to the world solid and positive scientific knowledge, founded on an extraordinary insight into nature and her operations, whilst the former has left it nothing but some poetical ideas with a farrago of nonsensical rubbish, such as hundreds of confessed madmen have written—is Emanuel Swedenborg. Still he was a man of great parts. In him were combined the opposite qualities of scientist, poet, and visionary. The desire of knowledge made him master the whole cycle of the sciences of his age, and when twenty-eight years old, he was one of the most learned men of his country. In 1716 he visited the English, Dutch, French, and German universities. In

1718 he transported a number of vessels over land from one coast to another. In 1721 he visited the mines of Europe, and wrote a description of them in his great work *Dœdalus Hyperboreus.* Then he gave himself up to theology, and unexpectedly turned to mysticism, often the denial of theology. He was fifty-five years old when he began to look within himself and to discover the wonders of the ideal world; after the mines of the earth, he explored the depths of the soul, and in this later exploration he forgot science. His pretended revelations drew upon him the hatred of the clergy; but he enjoyed such consideration in his own country that they could not injure him. At the Diet of 1751 Count Hopken declared that the most valuable writings on finance proceeded from the pen of Swedenborg. A mystical financier was what the world had never seen, and perhaps will never see again. He died in London. There is an English society which prints and circulates his works, filling about fifty large volumes; and he has many followers in this country. He moreover made many discoveries in astronomy, chemistry, and medicine; and was the forerunner of Gall in phrenology.

304. *His Writings and Theories.*—Much in his writings is no doubt absurd; but still we think a sense, not at once apparent, but which turns nonsense into sense, may be discovered therein. Whoso attentively reads the " New Jerusalem," or

the " Journey to the Astral Worlds," must see
that there is a hidden meaning in his abstruse language.   It cannot be assumed that a man who had
shown so much vigour of mind in his numerous
works on poetry, philosophy, mathematics, and
natural history—a man who constantly spoke of
" correspondences," wherein he attributed to the
least thing a hidden sense—a man whose learning
was unbounded and acute—that such a man wrote
without attaching some real meaning to his illusory
language.   The religion he professes is philan-
thropy, and consequently he gives to the abstract
idea of the perfect man the name of Man-God, or
Jesus Christ; those who aspire to it are angels and
spirits; their union becomes heaven, and the opposite, hell.

305. *Rationale of Swedenborg's Writings.*—From
the most remote antiquity we meet with institutions—as the foregoing pages have sufficiently
shown—ever aiming at political, religious, and
intellectual reform, but expressing their ideas by
speaking allegorically of the other world and the
life to come, of God and angels, or using archi-
tectural terms.   This practice, which is permanent and permeates all secret societies, aims at
morality in conduct, justice in government, general
happiness and progress, but aims at all these according to certain philosophical ideas, viz., that all men
are free and equal; but understanding that these

ideas, in the various conditions of actual society, in its different classes, and in the heads of government and worship, would meet with powerful opponents, it takes its phraseology from an imaginary world successfully to carry out its objects. Therefore its external worship resembles ours, but by the science of correspondences it becomes something different; which is thus expressed by Swedenborg: "There is in heaven a divine cultus outwardly similar to ours, but inwardly different. I was permitted to enter into the celestial temple (perhaps the lodge), where are shown the harmonized divinity and the deified humanity."

306. *The New Jerusalem.*—One of the chief conceptions of Swedenborg, as expounded in the " New Jerusalem," is the divine in the heart of every man, interpreted by humanity, which is one of the articles of faith of (true) Masonry. " To will and to do right without any interested aims, is to restore heaven in oneself, to live in the society of angels. The conscience of every man is the compendium of heaven ; all is there, the conception and sanction of all duties and all rights." It is thus Swedenborg speaks of the mystic or sectarian life: "Between the good and the evil there is the same difference that there is between heaven and hell. Those that dwell in evil and error resemble hell, because the love of hell is the opposite of that of heaven, and the two loves hate and make war upon each other unto death.

Man was created to live with the soul in the spiritual, and with the body in the natural, world. In every man, then, there are two individualities, the spiritual and the natural, the internal and the external. The internal man is truly in heaven and enjoys intercourse with celestial spirits, even during the earthly life, which is not the true, but only a simulated life. Man, being twofold, has two thoughts, the superior and the inferior, two actions, two languages, two loves. Therefore the natural man is hypocritical and false, for he is double. The spiritual man is necessarily sincere and true, because he is simple and one; in him the spirit has exalted and attracted the natural; the external has identified itself with the internal. This exaltation was happily attained to by the ancients, who in earthly objects pursued their celestial correspondences." He returns over and over again to the science of the correspondences, alluding to the initiations of the ancients, the true life that succeeds the simulated initiatory death, the mystical heaven which to the Egyptians and Greeks was nothing but the temple. " The science of the correspondences among the ancients was the highest science. The Orientals and Egyptians expressed it by hieroglyphics; which, having become unintelligible, generated idolatry. The correspondences alone can open the eyes of the mind, unveil the spiritual world, and make that apprehensible which does not come under the cognizance of the senses." Again he says: "I will show you what faith and charity are. Instead of faith and charity think of warmth and light, and you will understand all. Faith in its substance is truth, *i. e.* wisdom; charity in its essence is affection, *i. e.* love. Love and wisdom, or charity and faith, the good and the true, form the life of God in man." In the description of the fields of heaven, the guiding angel—perhaps the warden of the lodge—says to Swedenborg that the things around him are correspondences of the angelic science, that all he sees, plants, fruits, stones, all is corresponding, just as in masonic lodges. As there are three degrees in life, so there are three heavens, and the conditions of their respective inhabitants correspond with those of the initiated of the three masonic degrees. The "New Jerusalem" may be considered also as a protest against the papal rule, hated by Swedenborg, as by all sectaries. He sought its fate in the Apocalypse, as formerly did the Albigenses; and declared that the corrupt Roman clergy must make way for a better priesthood, and the decayed and idolatrous church for a new temple. To increase the authority of his words he adds: "What I tell you, I learned in heaven;" probably the sectarian heaven, into which he had been initiated. Extracts might be multiplied, but the above will suffice to show the spirit that animates the writings of Swedenborg; they will suffice to show that to enter into the hidden thoughts of most emblems, rites, and secret societies, it is necessary to consider the twofold and even threefold sense of the different figures. Every symbol is a mystery; nothing is done or said in secret assemblies that is not worthy of scrutiny— names, members, forms, all are indications, hints of hidden truths, dangerous truths, and therefore covered with double and triple veils.

307. *Various Swedenborgian Sects.*—From these writings arose various sects; one of them composed of men who await the New Jerusalem, believing in the marvellous prophecies, the conversations with angels, the seraphic marriages of the elect, and considering themselves the true disciples of Christ, because Swedenborg called the Sun of Mercy, which spreads light and warmth throughout the universe, the Saviour of the world. This sect has most followers in England. The other sects boast of possessing the greatest secrets of their master. Of these sects the following may be mentioned.

308. *Illuminati of Avignon.*—Pernetti, a Bene- dictine monk, and Gabrianca, a Polish nobleman and a mason, were the first to surround with whim- sical rites and ceremonies the knowledge and reve- ries of the Swedish mystic. In 1760 they established at Avignon a society of Illuminati, not to be con- founded with the Illuminati of Bavaria (316). The city of the popes became a sectarian stronghold, with affiliated lodges in the chief towns of France.

The members occupied themselves with philosophy, astronomy, and that social chymistry, which then subjected to a formidable examination all the elements of which political society is composed.

309. *Illuminated Theosophists.*—Paris wanted to have its own Swedenborgian rite, not satisfied with having introduced that of Pernetti. The Freemason Chartanier, who in 1766 was the master of the Parisian lodge " Socrates," modified the rite of Avignon, and called the new order the " Illuminated Theosophists," and after an active propaganda in France, crossed the Channel and opened a lodge in London, where at first he met with much success; but the rite was soon abandoned.

310. *Philosophic Scotch Rite.*—Another modification of the Avignon rite, was one introduced in 1770 by the Abbé Pernetti, who was entirely devoted to alchymy. He called the rite the " Hermetic " rite; but, as its name implies, it was more alchymistical than masonic. Boileau, a physician of Paris, and zealous follower of Pernetti, remodelled the Hermetic rite, rendered it more purely masonic, and gave it the name of the " Philosophic Scotch rite." The two rites were afterwards united into twelve degrees, the last of which is the " Sublime Master of the Luminous Ring," which boasted of being derived from Pythagoras. In 1780 an Academy of the Sublime Masters of the Luminous Ring was established in

France, the initiation into which consisted of the presumed philosophic doctrines of the sage of Samos.

311. *Rite of the Philalethes.*—Another rite founded on the masonic speculations of Swedenborg was one invented in the lodge of the " United Friends " in Paris. The members, among whom were Condorcet and Antoine Court de Gébelin, the author of the " Monde Primitif," called themselves " Philalethes," or " Searchers after Truth," and the founder was Lavalette de Langes, Keeper of the Royal Treasury. It was divided into twelve classes or chambers; the first six degrees were styled Petty, and the last six High Masonry. Like almost all societies founded on Masonry, the Philalethes endeavoured to lead man to his pristine virtue and liberty; they felt the approach of the Revolution, and kept themselves *au fait* of events and aspirations. The lodge of the *Amis Réunis*, the centre of the system, possessed a rich collection of works and MSS. on secret societies, a large chymical laboratory, a cabinet of natural history, all under the care of de Langes; but at his death, in 1788, the precious collection was dispersed and the lodge dissolved.

A lodge, in imitation of the above, was founded at Narbonne in 1780; but with considerable modifications. The brethren called themselves Philadelphians, who are not to be confounded with the Philadelphian Society founded in London about a century before, though they professed to derive their rites from England. They were divided into three categories or temples, and ten classes or circles. After the first three masonic degrees came the " Perfect Master," the " Elect," and the "Architect," forming the fourth. The fifth comprised the " Sublime Scotch ;" the sixth the " Knight of the East" and the " Prince of Jerusalem." The four remaining degrees were supposed to be the depositories of masonic knowledge, philosophical and physical, and of mystic science, fit to fortify and exalt the mind of man. These four degrees were called the first to the fourth chapters of Rose-Croix.

312. *Rite of Swedenborg.*—What is properly known as the rite of Swedenborg was another modification of the order of the Illuminati of Avignon (308), effected by the Marquis de Thome, in 1783, wherein he endeavoured to restore the true meaning of the doctrines of the Swedish mystic. It was a critical labour of some value, and the rite is still practised in several lodges of northern Europe. It consists of six degrees : Apprentice, Companion, Master Theosophite, Illuminated Theosophite, Blue Brother, Red Brother.

313. *Universal Aurora.*—In the same year, 1783, there was founded in Paris, the Order of the " Universal Aurora," whose chief object was the support of Mesmerism. Cagliostro took an active part in it.

III.

MARTINISM.

314.

ARTINEZ Paschalis.—The influence of the writings of Jacob Böhme, though perceptible in all mystic degrees founded since his day, is most visible in the mystic Masonry, called " Martinism," from its founder Martinez Paschalis, and its reformer the Marquis of St.-Martin, the " Unknown Philosopher." Martinez Paschalis was a Portuguese and a Jew, but having turned Christian after the manner of the Gnostics of the first centuries, he began in 1754 to assemble disciples in various French cities, chiefly Marseilles, Bordeaux, Toulouse, and Lyons, none of whom rose to the degree of epopt, or knew the secrets of the master, though he inspired all with the greatest respect and devotion towards himself. His secret doctrine appears to have been a confused medley of Gnosticism and Christianised Judaism, not excluding the cabala,

which in fact is found more or less in all theosophic
speculations, even in those of Böhme; though his
followers, as well as his opponents, from not understanding him, have attributed to him many erroneous
opinions which he never entertained. Paschalis laid
great stress on the omnipotence of will—this is a
point constantly insisted on, its truth being demon-
strated from the deepest ground, by Böhme. With
this writer he taught that intelligence and will are
the only active forces of nature, whose phenomena
man can control by willing energetically; and that
man in this manner can rise to the knowledge of the
supreme Ens. With these principles, Martinez condemned all empires founded on violence, and all
societies based on convention. He. longed for a
return to the patriarchal times—which the more
enlightened, however, look upon as times of rank
tyranny—and he also formed other conceptions
which we shall see more fully developed by the
Illuminati (316).

The life of Martinez, like his doctrines, is full of
gaps and mysteries. He arrived in a town no one
knew whence, he departed no one knew whither;
all at once he was seen where least expected. From
1768 to 1778 Paschalis resided either at Paris or
at Lyons. Then he suddenly crossed the ocean,
and died at St. Domingo in 1779. These sudden
appearances and disappearances were perhaps
needed to maintain his prestige. De Maître,

who had much intercourse with his disciples, states it for certain, that the order founded by him, and called the " Rite of the elected Cohens or Priests," had superior degrees, unknown to the members of the lower grades. We know the names of nine degrees, though not their rituals; they were :—Apprentice, Fellow-Craft, Master, Grand Elect, Apprentice Cohen, Fellow-Craft Cohen, Master Cohen, Grand Architect, Knight Commander. The zeal of some of the members, among whom we find Holbach, Duchamteau, and St. Martin, caused the order to prolong its existence some time after the death of the founder.

315. *Saint-Martin.*—We have seen that St.-Martin was a disciple of Paschalis ; he was also, for his day, a profound expounder of the doctrines of Böhme, some of whose works he translated. He to some extent reformed the rite of Paschalis, dividing it into ten degrees, classed in two temples. The first temple comprised the degrees of Apprentice, Fellow-Craft, Master, Ancient Master, Elect, Grand Architect, and Master of the Secret. The degrees of the second temple were Prince of Jerusalem, Knight of Palestine, and Knight of Kadosh. The order, as modified by him, extended from Lyons into the principal cities of France, Germany, and Russia. It is now extinct.

BOOK X.

ILLUMINATI.

" L'erreur et la vérité se partageaient l'empire de cette association, qui ne pouvait prospérer qu'en ces temps de demi-clarté, où les esprits vigoureux et les cœurs ardents sentent vivement la honte de l'esclavage religieux et politique, et ne trouvent pas de meilleurs moyens pour la combattre, que ceux qu'il emploie lui-même pour s'établir : la violence et la déception. . . . Dans ce nouveau tribunal secret des spectres hideux et menaçants apparaissaient au récipiendaire, et l'excitaient à la vengeance, au meurtre, à la trahison plus infâme."—RAGON.

AUTHORITIES.

Mirabeau. Histoire Secrète de la Cour de Berlin. 1789.
Luchet. Essai sur la Secte des Illuminés. Paris, 1789.
Robison. Proofs of a Conspiracy against all the Religions and Governments of Europe, carried on in the secret Meetings of Freemasons, Illuminati, and Reading Societies. London, 1797.

I.

SPARTACUS AND PHILO.

316.

FOUNDATION of Order.—Adam Weishaupt, a student in the University of Ingolstadt, learned and ambitious, and attracted by that love of mystery which is a prominent characteristic of youth, meditated the formation of a philosophico-political sect. When twenty-two years of age he was elected professor of Canon Law in the same University, a chair which had for twenty years been filled by the Jesuits; hence their rage against and persecution of Weishaupt, which he met boldly, returning hatred with hatred, and collecting partisans. The great aversion he then conceived for the Jesuits appears in many of the statutes of the order he founded. Jesuits, he often declares, are to be avoided like the plague. The sect of the Illuminati was founded in 1776, by Weishaupt, who adopted the pseudonym of *Sparta-*

cus; but it was years before its ritual and constitution were finally settled. Weishaupt, in order the better to succeed, connected himself with the Freemasons, by entering the lodge "Theodore of Good Counsel," of Eclectic Masonry, at Munich, and attempting to graft Illuminism on Freemasonry. Many members of the craft, misled by the construction of his first degrees, entered the order; but when they found that Weishaupt meant real work, and not mere play, they hung back. The society was instituted for the purpose of lessening the evils resulting from the want of information, from tyranny, political and ecclesiastical.

317. *Organisation.*—The society was by its founder divided into classes, each of which was again subdivided into degrees, in the following manner :—

Nursery	{	Preparation.
		Novice.
		Minerval.
		Illuminatus Minor.

Masonry	{	Symbolic	{	Apprentice.
				Fellow Craft.
				Master Mason.
		Scotch	{	Illuminatus Major, or Scotch Novice,
				Illuminatus Dirigens, or Scotch Knight.

Mysteries	{	Lesser.	{	Epopt, or Priest.
				Prince, or Regent.
		Greater	{	Magus, or Philosopher.
				Rex, King, Homme Roi, or Areopagite.

In the nursery and masonry degrees, the candidate was merely tried and prepared for the mystery degrees. If he was found unreliable, he was not allowed to go beyond; but if he proved an apt scholar, he was gradually initiated into the latter, where all that he had been taught before was overthrown, and radical and deistic theories and plans were unfolded, into the details of which it would be tedious to enter.

318. *Progress of Order.*—The most important person of the order after Weishaupt was Baron de Knigge, who assumed the pseudonym of "Philo." All the leading members equally adopted such pseudonyms. Thus we have seen that Weishaupt took the name of Spartacus, who in Pompey's time headed the insurrection of slaves; Zwack, a lawyer, was known among the initiated as "Cato;" Nicholai, bookseller, as "Lucian;" Professor Westenrieder, as "Pythagoras;" Canon Hertel, as "Marius;" and so on. The order made considerable progress, but some of its members betrayed its secrets, or as much of them as they knew. The Elector of Bavaria, in consequence, became alarmed at the political tenets taught in the assemblies of the Illuminati, and entirely suppressed the order in his territories.

319. *Secret Papers and Correspondence.*—It was only after the suppression of the order that the mode of initiation into the higher degrees and the true doctrines taught therein became known. A collec-

tion of original papers and correspondence was found, by searching the house of Zwack, in 1786. In the following year, a much larger collection was found at the house, of Baron Bassus, a member. From these we learn that one of the chief means recommended by the leaders for the success of the order was that of gaining over the women—not a bad plan. " There is no way of influencing men so powerfully as by means of the women," says the instructor. " These should, therefore, be our chief study. We should insinuate ourselves into their good opinion, give them hints of emancipation from the tyranny of public opinion, and of standing up for themselves; it will be an immense relief to their enslaved minds to be freed from any one bond of restraint, and it will fire them the more, and cause them to work for us with zeal," etc. Similar views are enunciated in a letter found among the correspondence:—" The proposal of Hercules (a member not identified) to establish a Minerval school for girls is excellent, but requires circumspection. . . . . We cannot improve the world without improving the women. . . . But how shall we get hold of them ? How will their mothers, immersed in prejudices, consent that others shall influence their education ? We must begin with grown girls. Hercules proposes the wife of Ptolemy Magus. I have no objection; and I have four step-daughters, fine girls. The eldest in particular is excellent. She is twenty-four, has read much, and is above all prejudices. They have many acquaintances. . . . It may immediately be a very pretty Society. . . . No man must be admitted. This will make them become more keen, and they will go much farther than if we were present. . . . Leave them to the scope of their own fancies, and they will soon invent mysteries, which will put us to the blush. . . . They will be our great apostles. . . . Ptolemy's wife must direct them, and she will be instructed by Ptolemy, and my step-daughters will consult with me. . . . But I am doubtful whether the association will be durable—women are fickle and impatient. Nothing will please them but hurrying from degree to degree . . . which will soon lose their novelty and influence. To rest seriously in one rank, and to be silent when they have found out that the whole is a cheat, (!) is a work of which they are incapable. . . . Nay, there is a risk that they may take it into their heads to give things an opposite turn, and then, by the arts in which they are adepts by nature, they may turn our order upside down." And a circumstance affecting the personal character of the founder, which was brought to light by the discovery of the secret correspondence, has contributed as much as anything else to give the order of the Illuminati a bad name. In the handwriting of Zwack were found a description of a strong box, which, if forced open, should blow up and destroy its contents; a recipe for sympathetic ink; how to take off impressions of seals, so as to use them afterwards as seals; a collection of some hundreds of such impressions, with a list of their owners; a set of portraits of eighty-five ladies in Munich, with recommendations of some of them as members of a lodge of sisters *illuminatæ;* injunctions to all superiors to learn to write with both hands, and to use more than one cypher; and other matters.

320. *Conclusion.*—The Society having been established in the small state of Bavaria, and so quickly suppressed, never made any lasting impression on the affairs of its own time, nor on those of the future. All the terrible effects attributed to its doctrines by Robison and other opponents of the order existed more in the imagination of the writers than in reality. If, as Robison says, the founders only wanted liberty to indulge their ambition and passions, they might, and, according to the secret correspondence quoted, seem to have done so, without the cumbrous machinery of a society whose members appeared so unmanageable. Weishaupt was deprived of his professor's chair, and banished from Bavaria, but with a pension of eight hundred florins, which he refused. He first went to Regensburg, and afterwards entered the service of the Duke of Saxe-Gotha. Zwack also was banished, and went into the service of the Prince of Salms, who soon after had so great a hand in the disturb-

ances in Holland. Of the Society of the Illuminati it may truly be said, that there was great cry and little wool; still it was not without its influence on the French Revolution.

BOOK XI.

BRIGANDAGE.

"La conquête de la totalité ou d'une partie d'un pays par un peuple étranger conduit naturellement au brigandage."—DEFAUCONPRET.

I.

THE CHAUFFEURS, OR BURNERS.

321.

RIGIN and Organization of Society.—The *Chauffeurs* or Burners formed a secret society formerly existing in France, and only extinguished at the end of the last century. Its members subsisted by rapine and murder. According to the slender notices we have of this society, it arose at the time of the religious wars which devastated France during the days of Henry III. and IV., and Catherine of Medici; and as the writers who searched into its history were Roman Catholics, they charitably assumed the original Chauffeurs to have been the defeated Huguenots, who took to this brigand life to avenge themselves on their conquerors. But the fact that the religious ceremonies of the society included the celebration of a kind of mass, strongly militates against this assumption of their origin. It is more probable that like similar fraternities formed in lawless times, it consisted of men dissatisfied with their lot, ordinary criminals and victims of want or injustice.

The Chauffeurs constituted a compact body, governed by a single head. They had their own religion, and a code of civil and criminal laws, which, though only handed down orally, was none the less observed and respected. It received into its fraternity all who chose to claim admission, but preferred to enrol such as had already distinguished themselves by criminal deeds. The members were divided into three degrees; the spies, though affiliated, did not properly form part of the society. The initiated were again subdivided into *decuriæ*, each with its *guapo* or head.

Though, as we have said, any one could be initiated, yet the society, like that of the Jesuits, preferred educating and bringing up its members. Whole families belonged to the fraternity, and the children were early taught how to act as spies, commit small thefts and similar crimes, which were rewarded more or less liberally, as they were executed with more or less daring or adroitness. Want of success brought proportionate punishment with it, very severe corporeal castigation, which was administered not merely as punishment, but also to teach the young members to bear bodily pain with fortitude. One would almost be inclined to think that those bandits had studied the code of Lycurgus! At the age of fourteen or fifteen the

boy was initiated into the first degree of the society.
At a kind of religious consecration he took an oath,
calling down on his own head the lightning and
wrath of heaven, if ever he failed in his duty towards the order. He received the sword he was to
use in self-defence and in fighting for his brethren.

The master had almost unbounded authority; he
kept the common purse, and distributed the booty
according to his own discretion. He also awarded
rewards or promotion, and inflicted punishment.
Theft from the profane, as outsiders were called, was
the fundamental law and, indeed, the support of the
society, but theft from a brother was punished, the
first time, by a fine three times the amount stolen.
When repeated, the fine was heavier, and sometimes the thief was put to death. Each brother
was bound to come to the assistance of another
when in danger; the honour of the wives of members was to be strictly respected, and concubinage
and prostitution were prohibited and severely
punished. Their mode of administering justice
was rational, *i. e.* summary. The accused person
was called before the general assembly of the members, informed of the charge against him, con-
fronted with the witnesses, and if found innocent
acquitted, if guilty he had either at once to pay the
fine imposed, receive the number of blows allotted,
or submit to hanging on the nearest tree, according
to the tenor of the sentence.

322. *Religious and Civil Ceremonies.*—The religious worship of the Chauffeurs was a parody on that of the church. The sermons of their preachers were chiefly directed to instructing them how most profitably to pursue their profession, and how to evade the pursuit of the profane. On fête-days the priests celebrated mass, and especially invoked the heavenly blessing on the objects and designs of the society. English navvies seem to have borrowed the leading feature of their marriage ceremony from that of the society of Chauffeurs, which was as follows: On the wedding-day the bridegroom and bride, accompanied by the best man and chief bridesmaid, presented themselves before the priest, who after having read some ribald nonsense from a dirty old book, took a stick, which he sprinkled with holy water, and after having placed it into the hands of the two chief witnesses, who held it up between them, he invited the bridegroom to leap over it, while the bride stood on the other side awaiting him. She received him in her arms, and held him up for a few moments before setting him down on the ground. The bride then went in front of the stick, and took her leap over it into the bridegroom's arms, whose pride it was to hold her up in the air as long as possible, before letting her down. Auguries were drawn of the future felicity and fecundity of the marriage from the length of time the bride had been able to hold up

her spouse, whilst both seated themselves on the stick, and the priest put on the bride's finger the wedding-ring. The navvies' ceremony therefore of "jumping over the broomstick" is no new invention.

Divorces were granted not only for proved or suspected infidelity, but also on account of incompatibility of temper—which proves the Chauffeurs to have been, in this respect at least, very sensible people—after the priest had tried every means to bring about a reconciliation. The divorce was pronounced in, public, and its principal feature was the breaking of the stick on which the pair had been married, over the wife's head. After that, each was at liberty to marry again.

323. *The Grand Master.*—The sect was spread over a great part of north-western France; made use of a peculiar patois, understood by the initiated only, and had its signs, grips and passwords like all other secret societies. It comprised many thousand members. Its existence and history first became publicly known through the judicial proceedings taken against it by the courts of Chartres, during the last decade of the preceding century. Many mysterious robberies, fires and murders were then brought home to the Chauffeurs. Its Grand Master at the time was Francis the Fair, so called on account of his singular personal beauty. Before his initiation he had been imprisoned for robbery

with violence, but managed to escape; the order sought him out and enrolled him amongst its members, and at the death of their chief, John the Tiler, unanimously elected him in his place. Taken prisoner at the above-mentioned period, he again found means to give his jailors at Chartres the slip— probably with their connivance—and was not heard of again. A rumour was indeed current at the time that he had joined the *Chouans*, and eventually perished, a victim to his debaucheries. Some hundreds of Chauffeurs were executed at Chartres; but the mass of them made their escape and swelled the ranks of the above-named *Chouans*.

It was chiefly during the Reign of Terror that the Chauffeurs committed their greatest ravages. At night large bands of them invaded isolated houses and the castles of the nobility, robbing the rich and poor alike. During the day children and old women, under various disguises and pretences penetrated into the localities, where property worth carrying off might be expected to exist, and on their reports the society laid its plans. Sometimes, disguised as national guards, they demanded and obtained admission in the name of the law. If they met with resistance they employed violence, if not they contented themselves with robbery. But sometimes they suspected that the inmates of the dwelling they had invaded concealed valuables; in that case they would tie their hands behind their backs and casting them on the ground apply fire to their feet—whence the name *chauffeurs*, " burners"—until they revealed the hiding-places of their treasures, or died in frightful agony. Such as did not die, were generally crippled for life.

324. *Discovery of the Society.*—A young man who had suffered in this fashion from some of the members of the society, determined to be revenged on them, by betraying them into the hands of justice. He revealed his plan to the authorities of Chartres and then set about its execution. In broad daylight in the market-place of Chartres he picked the pocket of a gendarme. The gendarme, having his instructions, of course saw nothing, but a *chauffeur*, some of whom were always prowling about, noticed the apparently daring deed, and reported it to his fellows and to his chief. That so clever and bold a thief should not belong to the brotherhood seemed unnatural; very soon therefore he was sought out and very advantageous offers were made to him if he would join them. At first he seemed disinclined to do so, but eventually yielded, and then showed all the zeal usual with neophytes. He attended all the meetings of the society, and speedily made himself acquainted with all their secrets; their signs, pass-words, modes of action, hiding-places, &c. Their safest retreat and great depot, where the booty was stored, was a wild wood in the neighbourhood of Chartres.

When the false brother had made these discoveries, and had also ascertained a day when nearly all
the members of the society would be assembled on
the spot for planning an expedition, he managed
to evade their vigilance, hastened to Chartres and
gave the necessary information to the authorities,
who had held a large number of men in readiness
in the expectation of this chance. These were at
once dispatched to the locality indicated by the
guide, the wood was surrounded, and the Chauffeurs
being taken unawares, either perished fighting or
were taken prisoners. Some of them managed to
escape, spread the alarm among members living
in other parts of the country, and the society was
for ever broken up.

II.

THE GARDUNA.

325.

RIGIN of the Society.—When that super-stitious bigot and tyrant Ferdinand, king of Spain—who believed himself a clever diplomatist, but was all his lifetime but the tool of a rapacious and bloodthirsty priesthood, the same who made the Inquisition all-powerful in Spain, and caused Columbus to be brought home in chains from the world he had dis-covered and added to the monster's dominions—when he resolved on the extermination in his king-dom of Moors and Jews—the former the most civilized and the latter the most industrious of his subjects—all the vagabonds and scoundrels of Spain were welcome to take part in the holy war, solely begun and carried on to extirpate heresy and spread the pure faith—at least such was the pre-tence. There had indeed, long before Ferdinand's time, been bands of malefactors, who roamed over the Spanish territory, and with the secret support

of the Roman Catholic clergy, who shared the
spoil, committed wholesale burglaries in the houses
of Moors and Hebrews, occasionally burning a re-
sisting heretic in the flames of his own house, as a
sweet-smelling savour unto Heaven.   The Moors
were enemies to their country though they had
civilized it, and the Jew belonged to an accursed
race ; to fight and destroy them was a meritorious
work which had the full approbation of the Church.
In Ferdinand's time the brigands readily joined
the crusade against the Moors; the king's motto
evidently was :

> " It is the sapiency of fools
> To shrink from handling evil tools ; "

and brigands may make good soldiers.   Brigands
moreover are generally well disposed towards the
Church, and submissive to the priest, and these
dispositions, so well agreeing with those of Ferdinand himself, could not but render the brigands
favourites with him.   But when the object of Ferdinand's holy war was attained, and the Moorish
power destroyed, he left the free-lances to shift for
themselves, which they did in their fashion, by returning to their former occupation of brigandage.
Now, although during the much vaunted reign of
Ferdinand the Catholic, as lying and servile writers
have called him, and Isabella, who was too much
under the influence of a set of demons in priestly

garb, and hence did all she could to increase the power of the Inquisition, nearly two millions of subjects—Moors and Jews—were driven from the realm, yet a great many remained who belonged to the one or the other race, and had, in order to be allowed to stay in their native country, adopted the Christian faith. Yet with such contempt were they looked upon by the genuine Spaniards, that they never spoke of them but as *marranos,* hogs, though many of them were the heads of, or belonged to, rich and influential families. The king and his Satanic crew of inquisitors were ever anxious to convict such persons of having relapsed into heresy, in order to burn them at the stake and confiscate their property. The brigands, well aware of this, selected the houses of the *marranos* for the scenes of their operations, and as long as a good share of the booty passed into the hands of priests, inquisitors, and the royal exchequer, Justice winked at the proceedings. But when the brigands grew tired of these heavy exactions, and refused to pay tribute, Justice suddenly woke up and resolved on exterminating the brigands, who snatched away spoil which legitimately belonged to the king and Inquisition, as the reward of their virtue in rigorously putting down heresy. It was then—when gendarmes and soldiers were sent out in all directions to catch or disperse the bands of brigands that infested the country—that these bands, which had hitherto acted independently of each other, determined for their greater safety to unite and form one large secret society. It was thus the *Garduna* arose, which soon provided itself with the whole apparatus of secret signs, passwords, initiatory ceremonies, and all other stage " property," necessary in such cases. Their connection with the Holy Inquisition was not severed thereby, but established on a business-like footing, though of course it remained secret—a sort of sleeping partnership. With such high protection at Court and in the Church, it is not surprising that the association soon counted its thousands of members, who actually made Seville their head-quarters, where all great plundering, burning, and murdering expeditions were planned and prepared.

326. *Organization.*—The society had nine degrees, arranged in three classes. To the inferior classes belonged the novices or *Chivatos* (roe-bucks), who performed the menial duties, acted as explorers and spies, or carried the booty; the *Coberteras* (covers), abandoned women who insinuated themselves into private houses to spy out opportunities for stealing, or acted as decoy-ducks, by alluring men into retired places, where they were set upon, robbed, and frequently murdered by the brigands. Lastly the *Facelles* (bellows), or spies, chiefly old men of what is called venerable appearance—whatever that may mean—sanctimonious in

carriage, unctuous in speech, haunting churches, in fact, saints. These not only disposed of the booty already obtained, but by their insinuating manners and reputation for piety wormed themselves into the secrets of families which were afterwards exploited for the benefit of the band. In the next class were the *Floreadores* (athletes), men stained with every vice, chiefly discharged or escaped convicts from the galleys, or branded by the hand of the executioner, whose office consisted in attacking and robbing travellers on the high road. Then came the proud *Pontsadores* (pinkers, *i. e.* bullies, expert swordsmen), sure to kill their man. Above these were the *Guapos* (heads, chiefs), also experienced duellists, and generally appointed to lead some important enterprise. The highest class embraced the *Magistri*, or priests, who conducted the initiations, preserved the laws, usages, and traditions of the society. The *Capatazes* (commanders), who resided in the different provinces through which the Garduna was spread, represented the *Hermano Mayor* or Grand Master, who exercised arbitrary and absolute power over the whole society, and ruled the members with a rod of iron. Strange that men, who will not submit to legitimate authority, yet will bow to and be tyrannized over by a creature of their own setting up! The Thugs, Assassins, Chauffeurs, and all similar lawless societies, surrendered their will to that of one man, in blind and slavish fear; but perhaps this is the only condition on which such societies can exist.

327. *Spirit of the Society.*—The Thugs or Assassins killed to rob, but the Garduna, having learnt its business so to speak in a more diabolical school, that of the Holy Inquisition, considered itself bound to perform any kind of crime that promised a chance of gain. The priests had drawn up a regular tariff, at which any number of members of the society could be hired to do any deed of darkness. Robbery, murder, mutilation, false evidence, falsification of documents, the carrying off of a lady, getting your enemy taken on board a ship and sold as a slave in a foreign colony—all these could be had "to order;" and the members of the Garduna were exceedingly conscientious and prompt in carrying out such pleasant commissions. One-half of the price paid for such services was generally paid on giving the order, and the other half on its completion. The sums thus earned were divided into three parts; one part went into the general fund, the other was kept in hand for running expenses, and the third went to the members who had done the work. That for a considerable period the affairs of the society were in a very flourishing state, is proved by the fact that they were able to keep in their pay at the Court of Madrid persons holding high positions to protect and further the interests of the members. They even had their

secret affiliates among judges, magistrates, governors of prisons and similar officials, whose chief duty lay in facilitating or effecting the escape of any member of the society that might have fallen into the hands of justice.

328. *Signs, legend, &c.*—It was mentioned above that the Garduna had its signs and passwords of recognition. When a Garduno found himself in the company of strangers, to ascertain if a brother was present, he would as it were accidentally put his right thumb to his left nostril; if a brother was present, he would approach him and whisper the pass-word, in reply to which another pass-word would be given; then, to make quite sure, there would be grips and signs, *à la* Freemason, and the two might talk at their ease in a jargon perfectly unintelligible to outsiders on their mutual affairs and interests. Their religious rites—and the Garduna insisted much on being a religious society— were those of the Papal Church, and as that Church is founded on legends innumerable, so the Garduna had *its* legend, which was as follows :—" When the sons of Beelzebub (the Moors) first invaded Spain, the miraculous Madonna of Cordova took refuge in the midst of the Christian camp. But God, to punish the sins of his people, allowed the Moors to defeat the orthodox arms, and to erect their throne on the broken power of the Christians, who retreated into the mountains of Asturia, and there

continued, as well as they could, their struggle with the enemies of God and oppressors of their country. The Madonna, daily and hourly implored by the faithful, granted some successes to their arms, so that they were not entirely destroyed, according to Heaven's first decree. And though they could not drive the Moors from Spain, they yet amidst the mountains preserved their religion and liberty. There lived at that time in the wilds of Sierra Morena an old anchorite, named Apollinare, vulgarly called Cal Polinario, a man of austere habits, great sanctity, and a devout worshipper of the Virgin. To him one morning the Mother of God appeared and spoke thus :—" Thou seest what evil the Moors do to thy native country and the religion of my Son. The sins of the Spanish people are indeed so great as to have excited the wrath of the Most High, for which reason he has allowed the Moors to triumph over you. But while my Son was contemplating the earth, I had the happy inspiration to point out to him thy many and great virtues, at which his brow cleared up ; and I seized the instant to beseech him by means of thee to save Spain from the many evils that afflict it. He granted my prayer. Hear therefore my commands and execute them. Collect the patriot and the brave, lead them in my name against the enemy, assuring them that I shall ever be by their side. And as they are fighting the good fight of the faith, tell them that even now they shall have their reward, and that they may in all justice appropriate to themselves the riches of the Moors, in whatever manner obtained. In the hands of the enemies of God wealth may be a means of oppressing religion, whilst in those of the faithful it will only be applied to its greater glory. Arise, Apollinare, inspire and direct the great crusade; I invest thee with full power, anointing thee with celestial oil. Take this button, which I myself pulled off the tunic of my celestial Son; it has the property of multiplying itself and working miracles without number; whoso wears one on his neck will be safe from Moorish arms, the rage of heretics and sudden death.' And the Virgin having anointed him and given him the button, disappeared, leaving an ambrosial flavour behind." Then the anchorite founded the *Holy* Garduna, which thus could claim a *right divine* to robbery and murder. Hence also no important predatory expedition was undertaken without a foregoing religious ceremony; and when a discussion arose as to how to attack a traveller, or to commit some other similar crime, the Bible was ostensibly referred to for guidance.

329. *Suppression of the Society.*—The laws of the society, like those of nearly all secret societies, were not written down, but transmitted by oral tradition, but the Garduna kept a kind of chronicle in which its acts were briefly recorded. This book, which

now lies in the archives of the tribunals of Seville, and which, with other documents, was seized in the house of the Grand Master Francis Cortina in 1821, formed the basis of the indictment of the society before the courts of justice. From this it appeared that the Garduna had its branches in Toledo, Barcelona, Cordova, and many other Spanish towns. It also revealed their close connection with the Holy Inquisition up to the seventeenth century. Of their list of crimes, the carrying off of women, chiefly at the instigation of the holy fathers of the Inquisition, forms about one-third, assassinations form another third, whilst robbery, false testimony, or denunciation, complete the list. The book further was the means of enabling the authorities to arrest many of the members of the society, who were tried without delay, and on the 25th November, 1822, the last Grand Master and sixteen of his chief followers expiated their crimes on the scaffold erected in the market-place of Seville, and the Garduna only survives in the bands of brigands who are yet to be occasionally encountered in the recesses of the Spanish mountains.

BOOK XII.

FELLOW-CRAFTS.

AUTHORITIES.

Perdiguier Agricola. Le Livre du Compagnonnage. Paris, 1840.

Moreau. Un Mot sur le Compagnonnage. Auxerre, 1841.

Giraud. Réflexions sur le Compagnonnage. Lyon, 1847.

Sand. Le Compagnon du Tour de France.

Sciandro. Le Compagnonnage, ce qu'il a été, ce qu'il est, etc. Marseilles, 1850.

Grimm. Altdeutsche Wälder. Cassel, 1813.

Brentano. Arbeitergilden der Gegenwart. Leipsic, 1871.

I.

FRENCH WORKMEN'S UNIONS.

330.

ORGANIZATION of Workmen's Unions.
—The origin of corporations of artisans
dates from the day in which the oppressed workers and neglected burghers
wished to resist feudal rapine, assure to themselves
the fruit of their own labour, increase their trade,
enlarge their profits, and establish friendly relations.
But whilst these ancient corporations rose up against
the aristocracy of blood and wealth, they did not
steer clear of the oligarchic spirit. In the first centuries of the Middle Ages, the journeyman did not
separate from his master; he lived and worked with
him. There did not then exist that distinction which
afterwards displayed itself so openly—in fact, even
now, in many German towns the journeymen eat at
the master's table. Then the journeyman was to the
master what the squire was to the knight; and as the
squire could be received into the ranks of knighthood,

so the apprentice, at the end of his term, could establish himself as master. But by-and-bye it did not suffice to possess property or skill, to become a master; it became necessary after the apprenticeship to travel for two or three years, the object of which was, and still is, to acquire greater skill, and a knowledge of the various modes of working in different towns, adopted in the particular trade to which the journeyman belonged. On his return, he had to make his master-piece; if approved by a committee of masters, he was received among them; if not, he was rejected, and was not allowed to work on his own account. Thus the masters had in their turn transformed themselves into an aristocracy hostile to the majority, speculating on, rather than administering to, the common labour, their interests being opposed to those of the workmen. The ostracism which thus pursued the great army of labourers, and the segregation to which they were condemned, necessarily produced a reaction, which, unable to have recourse to open revolt, assumed the form of a secret sodality, with rites and customs peculiar to itself. The workman, moreover, unlike the master, was not tied to any city or country, but could wander from place to place—a life which, in fact, he must prefer to staying for ever in one workshop or factory, where the experience needed for the mastership could not be attained. Hence arose the ancient custom of the " Tour of France " and the multiform *compagnonnage*, which, whilst a source of pleasure

to the workmen settled in a town, became a necessity for the travelling, the persecuted journeyman;
who thus withdrew himself from under the regular
legislation, which only protected the manufacturer,
and joined, as it were, a subterranean association to
protect himself and his affiliates from the unpunished
injuries inflicted on them by burghers and masters.

331. *Connection with Freemasonry.*—Freemasonry
was early mixed up with the *compagnonnage,* and the
construction of the Temple, which is constantly met
with in the former, also plays a great part in the
latter—a myth, undefined, chronologically irrecon-
cilable, a poetic fiction, like all the events called
historical that surround the starting-points of various sects; for sects, existing, as it were, beyond
the pale of official history, create a history of their
own, exclusive of, and opposed to, the world of facts,
like the genius of Shakspeare, that cares little for
geography or chronology, but whose grand anachron-
isms belong to a higher truth, a more intrinsic reality
—the truth and reality of art. The Solomon of the
legend, so different from that of the Bible, is one of
the patriarchs of the *compagnonnage;* and, like the
masonic ceremonies, the rites of these journeyman
associations continually allude to that *moral* archi-
tecture, that proposes to erect prisons for vice, and
temples to virtue. Further, and in the same way,
the embraces and kisses of the craftsmen remind us
of the symbolic grips of the Freemasons, and the
brotherly kiss of ancient knighthood.

332. *Decrees against Workmen's Unions.*—We are often obliged to seek for information concerning secret societies in clerical invectives and judicial prosecutions; these are lamps shedding a sinister light on associations whose existence was scarcely suspected. Thus *compagnonnage* existed before Francis I.; for this king, though he protected the Carbonari (348-364), and actually introduced the Carbonari term of "cousin" into the language of Courts, issued an edict against the former, forbidding journeymen to bind themselves with oaths; to elect a chief; to assemble in greater numbers than five in front of the workshops, on pain of being imprisoned or banished; to wear swords or sticks in the houses of their masters or the streets of the city; to attempt any seditious movement; or to hold any banquet at the beginning or the end of an apprenticeship. A subsequent regulation, A. D. 1723, prohibits any community, confraternity, assembly, or cabala of workmen; and a parliamentary decree of 1778 renews the prohibition, and enjoins on tavern-keepers not to receive into their houses assemblies of more than four craftsmen, nor in any way to favour the practices of the pretended *devoir* (duty). The language of the clergy is equally energetic. A deliberation of the Parisian clergy of 1655 says: "This pretended *devoir* consists in three precepts—to honour God, protect the property of the master, and succour the companions. But these companions

dishonour God, profane the mysteries of our religion, ruin the masters, withdrawing the workmen from the workshop, when some of those inscribed in the ' cabala' complain of having been injured. The impieties and sacrileges they commit vary according to the different trades; but they have this in common, that before being received into the association, every member is bound to swear on the Gospel that he will not reveal either to father or mother, wife or son, either to cleric or layman, what he is about to do or will see done; and for this purpose they choose an inn, which they call the mother, wherein they have two rooms, in one of which they perform their abominable rites, whilst in the other they hold their feasts." Even before 1645, the clergy had denounced the tailors and shoemakers to the authorities of Paris for dishonest and heterodox practices, and the faculty of theology had prohibited the pernicious meetings of workmen, under pain of the greater excommunication; so that the companions, to escape ecclesiastical persecution, held their meetings in those purlieus of the Temple which enjoyed the right of sanctuary. Even thence they were removed, however, by the decree of the 11th September, 1651.

333. *Traditions.*—In assuming the denomination of " duty," the companions wished to intimate that they imposed on themselves duties and laws. They recognised three founders—Solomon, master James,

and father Soubise. Solomon built the temple; James was said to be the son of a famous architect, Joachim, born at St. Romily. James, having gone to Greece, heard the summons of Solomon, and went to him; and, having received from Hiram the order to erect two columns, he acquitted himself with such zeal and skill, that he was at once made a master and the companion of Hiram. The temple being finished, he returned again to Gaul with master Soubise, who had been his inseparable companion at Jerusalem. However, the pupils of master Soubise, jealous of James, attempted to assassinate him, and the latter threw himself into a marsh, where the reeds supported and concealed him, saving his life; but eventually he was discovered by the pupils of Soubise, who was unaware of their nefarious design, and slain. Soubise long mourned James; and when his end approached, he taught the companions their " duties," and the mode of life they ought to pursue. Among the rites he placed the kiss of brotherly affection and the custody of a reed—the acacia of the Freemasons—in memory of James. A variation of this legend represents Soubise as an accomplice of the murder, and a suicide from desperation. The reader will at once see that this is the story of Hiram, nay, of Osiris, and all the great deities of antiquity, over again; in the Legend of the Temple (192), Solomon also is an accomplice in the murder of his architect.

334. *Branches and Degrees.*—Acknowledging three founders, the companions divided themselves into three main branches; the sons of Solomon, those of master James, and those of father Soubise. The sons of Solomon were descended from the ancient privileged building corporations, and from others not privileged, but employed on public works. They assumed different denominations, such as "wolves" (197), and *Gavots*, which latter designation they retained, because coming from Judæa to France, they landed on the coast of Provence, whose inhabitants are still called Gavots. The wolves (197), stonemasons, have two degrees, fellow-crafts and youths. The *Gavots*, carpenters and ironsmiths, are divided into three: accepted fellow-crafts; advanced fellow-crafts; and initiated fellow-crafts. They all commemorate the death of master Hiram.

335. *Various Associations.*—The sons of master James called themselves by various names, such as *Compagnons Passants, Dévorants,* &c. The sons of father Soubise were known as "Jovials, or Companions of the Foxes," or as *Drilles,* an ancient French word signifying "companions," and by that scarcely desirable one of "dogs," in commemoration, it is said, of the dog who discovered the body of Hiram. It is more probable, however, that this denomination had the same origin as that of "wolves," for which dogs may easily be mistaken; or

that it refers to the star Sirius (210), in which case
the name Soubise might be a corruption of the
epithet Sabazius, given to Bacchus (57). With
the second of these branches of companionship,
comprising at first the three trades of stone-mason,
locksmith, and joiner, and with the third, composed entirely of carpenters, were afterwards ·
affiliated other trades, such as those of turners,
glaziers, weavers, shoemakers, smiths, nailmakers,
hatters, bakers, tanners, plasterers, and others.
With these the probability and number of schisms
increased; and the families of the "Rebels," "Independents," "Foxes of Liberty," and others arose
almost as a natural consequence.

336. *General Customs.*—The square and compasses were the symbols of the *compagnonnage;*
the members called each other by the name of their
country, because every one carried his country with
him in himself, and found hospitality and assistance
among the brethren to whom he addressed himself. And the woman that entertained them in
their tour or wanderings through France, was
called by the endearing name of mother—and
truly the association was to them a mother, that
succoured them when they wanted bread, and
enabled them to refuse working for wages below
the custom of the trade; that recompensed the industrious and punished the worthless, so that
throughout France they were denounced and met

with no friendly reception. The aspirant for initiation was obliged to have finished his apprenticeship; he was instructed in the word, signs and grips, and attached a ribbon of a particular colour to his cap and button-hole; received a stick of a certain length, earrings that represented the square and compasses, and a mark on the arm and chest. Strange customs prevailed, and still do prevail in many parts of the Continent, as the writer knows from personal observation, at the setting out of a member for his wanderings. He was accompanied beyond the town by his friends, one of them carrying his knapsack, and another singing the parting song, in the chorus of which all joined. They also carried bottles of beer and cups. Arrived at a certain distance from the town, the beer was drunk and the bottles and cups were thrown into the neighbouring fields. In some trades they hung a bottle to a tree, to symbolize the death of Saint Stephen, all throwing stones at the innocent bottle, except he who was about to set out, and who took leave of his companions, saying :—" Friends, I take leave of you as the apostles took leave of Christ, when they set out to preach the gospel."

337. *Customs among Charcoal-burners and Hewers.* —St. Theobald is the patron of the charcoal-burners (349), one of the oldest trade corporations. There were three degrees, aspirant, master and hewer. The aspirant was called *guépier*. A white

tablecloth was spread on the ground, and a salt-
cellar, a cup of water, a lighted taper and a
crucifix placed on it.   The kneeling aspirant swore
on the salt and water faithfully to keep the secrets
of the association.   He was then taught the words
by which he could know, and make himself known
to, his brethren in the forest, as well as the symbolic
meaning of the objects before him—the tablecloth
signified the winding-sheet in which every man
shall be wrapped up; the taper, the lights burning
round the death-bed; the cross, man's redemption;
the salt, the theological virtues.   This ritual was
austere and sad, like the existence of the poor
charcoal-burners, whose joys are numbered, but
whose griefs and privations are endless; it prevailed
in the Jura, the Alps, and the Black Forest.   The
catechism of the hewers contains passages of pathetic
simplicity.   Segregated in the immense forest, they
fix their eyes on the heaven above and the earth
beneath; their religion bears a resemblance to that
of the pilots of Homer; earth and heaven, nature
and God, such is their worship, whence arises a
moral of tender and passionate fraternity.

" Q. Whence come ye, cousin of the oak ?

A. From the forest.

Q. Where is your father ?

A. Raise your eyes to heaven.

Q. Where is your mother ?

A. Cast your eyes on the earth.

Q. What worship do you pay to your father ?

A. Homage and respect.

Q. What things do you bestow on your mother ?

A. My care during life, and my body afterwards.

Q. If I want help, what will you give me ?

A. I will share with you half my day's earnings and my bread of sorrow; you shall rest in my hut and warm yourself at my fire."

How much resignation in this brief dialogue, how much warm affection! Another society of hewers, called the society of the " Prodigal Son," had a still more dismal ritual. Over three doors of a symbolic tower was written :—" The past deceives me ; the present tortures me ; the future terrifies me." A triangle with the letters S. J. P. reminded them of the wisdom of Solomon, the patience of Job, and the repentance of the Prodigal Son. On the white apron was represented a heart, surrounded with black, over which rolled a red tear, a tear of blood and despair. The pangs and wretchedness of life depressed the imagination of these poor woodmen ; still they had faith in Time as the repairer of all, and on one of their symbolic objects they wrote : *Le temps vient à bout de tout.* Another society, of which very little is known, called itself, *Moins diable que noir;* as if to indicate that the blackness of their outside did not prevent goodness of heart.

338. *Customs in various other Trades.*—The saddlers and shoemakers had their own initiatory practices. In the room where the initiation took place,

there arose a rough altar, on which were placed a crucifix, tapers, a missal, and whatever is necessary for the celebration of divine service. This was performed, many peculiar phrases being intermingled therewith; after which the neophyte was made acquainted with the rites of the *devoir*, the signs and passwords, and the symbolic meaning of the forms and jewels. The reception of the hatters in its purifications and funereal myth approached still nearer to the ancient initiations. A stage or dais was erected in a large hall; on the stage were placed a cross, a crown of thorns, a palm branch, and all the instruments of the Passion of Christ. Close by stood a large basin of water. The aspirant represented Christ, and passed through the various episodes of the Passion of the Redeemer; and finally knelt down before the basin, when the water, the baptism of regeneration, was poured on his head. No doubt the original institutors of this rite had honest and elevated views; but in course of time the whole degenerated into a farce *à la* Ran-Tan Club. In the reception of the tailors the candidate was led into a room, in the centre of which stood a table covered with a white cloth, whereon were placed a loaf of bread, a salt-cellar overturned, three sugar loaves, and three needles. He also passed through the various stages of the Passion of Christ. He was then conducted to a second room, where a banquet was prepared, and, as it is asserted, pictures were exhibited of the *vie galante* of three journeymen tailors, pleasing to the senses ; which may remind us of the peculiar worship entering into all the ancient mysteries.

339. *Heroes and Martyrs of the Institution.*— These initiations gave a certain importance to the various trade-unions and their members ; it was their common patrimony that kept up the *esprit de corps,* though it was not free from the arrogance and ex- clusiveness which multiplied rites, intolerance, jealousies and enmities, that periodically ended in sanguinary struggles—the tragic episodes of a drama, now barbaric, now heroic. Thus the *com- pagnonnage,* as it had its poets, so it had its martyrs, the victims of vulgar prejudices, who thought they were sacrificing themselves for the glory and power of the *devoir,* and whose song of death, though it breathed an implacable spirit of hatred, issued from their lips as the song of a just and meritorious war.

" Tous ces Gavots infâmes
Iront dans les enfers
Brûler dedans les flammes
Comme des Lucifers."

The disturbances at Lyons, Marseilles, Bordeaux, disgraced the *compagnonnage.* In the middle of the last century the rivalry between the two sections of the stone-masons of Lyons ended in the expulsion of one of them from that city, and their attempt to return led to the most terrible scenes of violence and bloodshed.

II.

GERMAN WORKMEN'S UNIONS.

340.

HUNTSMAN'S *Phraseology.*—In the woods infested by robbers we meet with the first germs of these corporations, with rough but characteristic customs. Charcoal-burners and hunters need means to recognise each other, so as not to shake hands with an enemy. Grimm has collected upwards of two hundred venatic terms and phrases. The questions and answers of the wandering journeymen have a great resemblance to those of hunters; the intonation is the same, and both make great use of the symbolic numbers three and seven. The formulæ necessarily have reference to the various incidents of the hunter's life.

" *Q.* Good huntsman, what have you seen to-day?

A. A noble stag and a wild boar; what can one desire better?

Q. Why do call yourself a master huntsman?

A. A brave huntsman obtains from princes and lords the title of master in the seven liberal arts. From these sentiments which ennoble the dignity of an art or trade there arises often that chivalrous love, which renders life gentle, and gives it an aim and a reward worthy of it.

Q. Tell me, good huntsman, where have you left the fair and gentle damsel?

A. I left her under a majestic tree, and am going to rejoin her. Long live the maid dressed in white that every morning brings me a day of good fortune. Every day I see her again at the same place; and when I am wounded she cures me, and says to me :— ' I wish the huntsman safety and happiness; may he meet with a fine stag ! ' "

341. *Initiation.*—Artisans, more closely united than hunters, did not admit new members into their sodality except after long and solemn trials; their catechisms breathe throughout a spirit of brotherly affection and attention to moral and civil duties. They were divided into degrees, and it is remarkable that the German workmen have long been accustomed to the word, sign, and grip of the Freemasons. The operative masons were divided into *Wort-Maurer* (Word Masons) and *Schrift-Maurer* (Writing or Diploma Masons). The former had no other proof to give of their having been regularly brought up to the trade of builders, but the word and signs; the latter had written indentures to show.

There were laws, enjoining master masons to give employment to journeymen who had the proper word and signs. Some cities in this respect possessed more extensive privileges than others. The word given at Wetzlar, entitled the possessor to work over the whole empire. With the German journeymen also the three years' travel in search of improvement is an universal condition, and the usual time for setting out is the spring. The *Handwerksbursche* is even now a German institution; though he is now not so frequently met with on the high-road, because railways enable him to travel more cheaply than he could on foot.

342. *Initiation of Cooper.*—Every trade again has its particular mode of initiation; but as there necessarily is a great similarity of ritual and ceremonies, their details would become a tedious repetition. I therefore confine myself to one craft—that of the cooper. Permission is first asked to introduce to the assembly of companions or fellow-crafts the youth who is to be made one of them, and who is called the "Apron of Goatskin." The companion who introduces him says:—" Some one, I know not who, follows me with a goatskin; a murderer of staves, a wood-spoiler, a traitor; he is on the threshold, and says he is not guilty; he enters, and promises, after having been 'put into shape' (*ébauché*) by us, to become a good journeyman." Leave having been given, the apprentice seats him-

self on a stool placed on a table, and the companions
try to upset him; but his guide keeps him up,
whereupon he is repeatedly baptized and consecrated
with beer. The patron then says:—" What do you
call yourself now? Choose a name, genteel, short,
and that pleases the girls. He that has a short
name pleases every one, and every one drinks a cup
of wine or beer to his health. . . . And now to pay
the expenses of the baptism, give what every one
else has given, and the masters and journeymen
shall be content with you." The candidate also
receives numerous instructions how to conduct himself on his wanderings. He is not to be deterred by
the difficulties that encounter him at the outset.
After having passed through a forest full of dangers,
he is supposed to arrive in a pleasant meadow, and
to behold a pear-tree full of tempting fruit. Is he
to lie down under it, and wait till the pears fall into
his half-open mouth? Is he to mount the tree?
No; the farmer or his men would see him, and give
him a beating. He is to shake the tree, and some
of the fruit will fall down, with which he is to
regale himself, leaving some on the ground for some
companion who may come after him, and perhaps
not be strong enough to shake the tree. Pursuing his
way, he comes to a torrent, over which the trunk of
a large tree serves for a bridge. There he encounters a young girl leading a goat. What shall
he do? Push the girl and the goat into the water,

and pass on? No; let him take the goat on his shoulder, the girl in his arms, and cross the bridge. He may afterwards marry the girl, because he needs a wife, and kill the goat for the nuptial feast, and the skin will make him a new apron. Arriving in a town, he is to go to the inn kept by a master; if his daughter shows him the way to his bedroom, he is to keep a guard over himself; and on the next day he is to go about looking out for work. Perhaps he will be offered it by three masters—the first is rich in wood and hoops; the second has three handsome daughters, and regales his workmen with plenty of wine and beer; the third is poor; with which one is he to accept work? With the first he would become a first-rate cooper; with the second he would be happy, having drink in plenty, and dancing with the charming girls; but with the third? He is to be as ready to work for the poor as for the rich master. This discourse, of which there is much more, being ended, the novice attempts to run into the street and cry fire! The companions restrain him, and copiously baptize him with cold water; and then, of course, follows a dinner.

343. *Curious Works on the Subject.*—There exist in Germany numerous works on the rites and customs of various traders; the following are some of them —" The Millers' Crown of Honour, or a Complete Description of the True Nature of the Circles of the Company of Millers. By a Miller's

Apprentice, George Bohrmann." We here get into masonic symbolism. One woodcut represents a circle with mystic sentences, and the explanation says that everything was created from or by the circle. Then there follows the history of bakers according to the Scriptures; then a poetically described journey, with particulars of the most celebrated mills of Lusatia, Silesia, Moravia, Hungary, Bohemia, &c. The names of the three most famous millers that, according to the author, ever existed, are placed in the form of a triangle; and the book concludes with an invocation to the Architect of the Universe. A work of a similar nature is entitled, " Customs of the Worshipful Trade of Bakers ; how every one is to conduct himself at the inn and at work. Printed for the use of those about to travel." Another is called, " Origin, Antiquity, and Glory of the Worshipful Company of Furriers ; an accurate Description of all the Formalities observed from time immemorial in the Initiations of Masters, and the manner of examining the Journeymen. The whole faithfully described by Jacob Wahrmund (True Mouth)." All the companies boast of their ancient descent, but none more than that of the Furriers, who claim that God Himself was at first one of their fellow-workers, seeing that the Bible says that God made aprons of skins for Adam and Eve—an honour shared by no other company.

344. *Raison d'être of the Compagnonnage.*—The

compagnonnage may be called an operative knighthood. Its rites, symbols, and traditions are only its tangible form. The necessity for workmen to find, on their arrival in a new town, a nucleus of friends, a rendezvous, a *mother*, in the midst of the exclusion into which the constituted trades corporations would have thrown them, was the *raison d'être* of these associations. The possibility of struggling by means of associative force and the passive resistance of numbers against the oppression of manufacturers, and of equalizing forces otherwise disproportionate, was a further cause of these sodalities. In the Middle Ages, in which the central power was barely sufficient to oppress, but did not avail to protect, and when the individual was exposed to arbitrary treatment, and deprived of all means of defence, secret associations on behalf of justice necessarily arose in many countries, Holy Vehms providing for public security.

345. *Guilds.*—The Guilds had the same origin, but can scarcely be reckoned among secret societies, though their influence was often secretly exercised ; and kings frequently turned them to account in their opposition to the aristocracy, as, for instance, Louis the Fat, who was himself the founder of an association called the " Popular Community," intended to put a stop to the brigandage of the feudal lords, whose castles were in many instances but dens of thieves. In England, the first guilds

of which clear records have been preserved, were established in the eleventh century. By the laws of guilds, no person could work at a trade who had not served a seven years' apprenticeship to it. But with the introduction of machinery, this custom gradually fell into disuse, as the small or retail manufacturers of olden times became less and less, and the relations between employers and their workmen were changed—relations such as may even yet be found to exist in some places in Germany and Switzerland, where one master keeps an apprentice and from two to four workmen. This style of industry might be found not many years ago in Yorkshire among the small cloth-manufacturers. This quiet industry was broken up by the rapid introduction of machinery. The small men, indeed, sought to defend themselves by insisting on old trade regulations, but without success; for in 1814 every vestige of the old trade regulations had disappeared from the English statute-books. The Coalition Act of 1800, not repealed till 1824, often compelled the workmen who thus combined to assume the character of members of Friendly Societies. Their main objects were to prevent the employment of women and children in the immense factories everywhere springing up, and to enforce the old law of apprenticeship. Failing in these objects, they next resorted to strikes, with the nature, operation, and effects of which every one is familiar.

II.   G

346. *German Students.*—A fellowship of a very different kind, but still a *compagnonnage,* is that of the students at German Universities, to which a few lines may therefore be devoted. The student or *Bursch* looks upon the inhabitants of the town, whose university he honours with his presence, as " Philistines ;" and town and gown rows are as usual in Germany as in this country. All non-students are Philistines, whether they be kings, princes, nobles, or belong to the *canaille.* The students form two grand associations, the *Burschen-schaften,* consisting of students from any state; and *Landsmannschaften,* composed of students of the same state only. Each has its own laws, regulations, and officers, ruling according to a charter; but all members of the universities acknowledge moreover a general code, called the " Commentary." Such as refuse to belong to one of these associations are held in very slight estimation, and are called by all kinds of opprobrious names, such as *Kameele* (camels), *Finken* (fitches), and others more offensive. The collegiate students (sizars), called *Frösche* (frogs), cannot take part in the meetings of the *Burschen.* The freshman is a *Fuchs* (fox), or also a *Goldfuchs* (golden fox), because he has still a few gold coins; after six months he is a *Brandfuchs* (burnt fox), and his arrival at that state is celebrated with ridiculous ceremonies. In the second year the *Brandfuchs* rises to the dignity of *Jungbursch* (young Bursch) ; in the

third he becomes an *Altbursch* (old Bursch), *altes Haus* (old house), or *bemoostes Haupt* (mossy head). Students who are natives of the university town are called *Ourds*, because their mothers can send them, if they please, a dish of that article of food for their suppers. To rise from one degree to another the *Fuchs* has to go through a series of probations, especially putting to the test his powers of drinking and smoking. On his first visit to the *Oommershaus*, commerce house, as the tavern which the students patronize is called, he is unfailingly made drunk, at his own expense, and while at the same time entertaining all the "old houses." The next morning he awakes with the *Katzenjammer* (cat's lamentation). He dresses in a fantastic style, wearing a Polish jacket, jack-boots with spurs, and a cap of the colour of the society to which he belongs ; to his buttonhole is attached an enormous tobacco pouch ; in his mouth he carries a long pipe, and an ironshod stick in his hand. He endeavours above all things to become a *flotter Bursch*, a student *de pur sang*, and is proud if an "old house" makes him his *Leibfuchs* (favourite fox). The Philistine who offends the students is condemned to the *Verruf* (outlawed); and frequently the students have turned out against the citizens, forming with their *Stiefelwichser* (bootcleaners, or gyps), an array not to be despised by the military. The cry of *Burschen 'raus!* students turn out ! would send terror through the small peaceable towns of Germany. Sometimes they would punish the town by leaving it in a body, and only return on their terms being agreed to. Such emigrations took place at Göttingen in 1823; at Halle in 1827; and at Heidelberg in 1830. A few details of these "emigrations" may be amusing. On the last-named occasion the students, who had again secretly formed a *Burschenschaft,* put under the ban the Museum of that town, because the rules for its management displeased many of them. For this the ringleaders were seized and brought to trial. But on the cry of *Burschen 'raus !* all the students, hastily snatching up what articles they most needed, threw them into chaises, on horses, on the backs of the shoe-blacks, and marched out of the town to Schwelzingen ; and it was only when their demands with regard to the Museum were conceded, that they returned to Heidelberg. Another marching forth had occurred many years before. A student, as he went past the watch-house, forgot to take the pipe from his mouth. Thereupon arose a contention between him and the soldier on guard ; the latter called an officer, by whom the student was grossly insulted. This gave occasion to an " emigration," which however proceeded no further than to a place about a mile from the city, whence the students at once returned, all their demands being conceded ; which were that a full amnesty should be granted for all that had passed and the soldiers removed. Moreover the military were obliged to post themselves on the bridge, the officers at their head, and to present arms, while the students marched past in triumph, with music playing before them. But though the German student would thus seem to think of nothing but smoking his pipe, to which he gives the elegant name of *Stinktopf,* drinking unlimited quantities of wine, beer and punch, entertaining the daughters of the cits, which daughters he gallantly calls *Geier* (vultures), whilst *grisettes* are *Besen* (brooms), running into debt, fighting duels—to be called *dummer Junge* (stupid youngster), is an insult which necessitates a challenge—and generally ruining his health, yet when he buckles to work he will accomplish mental feats that would astonish many an Oxford first-class man, or Cambridge wrangler. Out of all this fermentation and froth there comes at last good wine, and all the intellectual greatness of Germany, and much of its political progress, are due to the roistering *Burschen,* of whom I cannot speak but with a kind of sneaking kindness, retaining many pleasant personal recollections of them.

347. *Ancient custom of Initiation.*—In the following passage, taken from the "History of the High School of Königsberg," by Arnold, the reader may detect many customs analogous to those practised in the initiations to the ancient mysteries, as prevailing so late as the first half of the seventeenth

century at the matriculations of German students. "In the university where the deposition was customary, the newly-arrived student, the so-called 'Brane' or Bacchant, announced himself to the dean of the philosophical faculty, and prayed that he might through the deposition be received among the students. When the Branen amounted to a certain number the dean appointed a day on which to celebrate the deposition; and summoned, besides the Branen, the depositor with his instruments, and an amanuensis. They appeared on the appointed day before the dean; the depositor in the first place put on a harlequin's dress, caused the Branen to attire themselves in the same style, and put on them other ludicrous articles of dress, especially hats and caps with horns, and distributed amongst them the instruments with which the deposition should be executed—coarse wooden combs, shears, axes, hatchets, planes, saws, razors, looking-glasses, stools, and so on. The depositor then marshalled the Branen in rank and file, placed himself at their head, and conducted them to the hall, where the deposition should be performed, and there addressed a speech to the dean and the spectators, who consisted of students. The depositor commenced the deposition by striking the Branen with a bag filled with sand or bran, and compelling them to scamper about with all manner of laughable gestures and duckings in order to escape the strokes of the sand-bag. He then propounded to them certain questions or riddles, and they who did not answer them quickly received so many strokes with the sand-bag, that the tears often started from their eyes. The Branen then gave up the instruments which they had held in their hands, and laid down on the ground, so that their heads nearly touched each other. The depositor then planed their shoulders, filed their nails, pretended to bore through and saw off their feet, hewed every limb of their bodies into shape, knocked off their goat's horns and tore out of their mouths with a pair of great tongs the satyr's teeth stuck in on purpose. The Branen were then caused each to sit on a stool with only one leg. The depositor then put on them a dirty napkin, soaped them with brick-dust, or with shoe blacking, and shaved them so sharply with a wooden razor that the tears often started from their eyes. The combing with the wooden combs was equally rough, and after the combing their hair was sprinkled with shavings. After all these operations the depositor with his sand-bag drove them out of the hall, took off his grotesque attire, put on his proper costume and commanded the Branen to do the same. He then reconducted them to the hall and commended them in a short Latin speech to the dean, who replied also in Latin, explaining the custom of deposition and adding much good advice. Finally, he gave to each of them, as a symbol of wisdom, a few grains of salt to taste, scattered in sign of joy some drops of wine over their heads, and handed to them the certificate of the accomplished deposition.

It is scarcely necessary to point out the analogies between the above initiation into student life and that into the ancient mysteries and modern Freemasonry; the disguises, trials, addresses, and whole ceremonial, are all on the model of the secret society.

Hoffmann's *Lebens-Ansichten des Katers Murr,*—"Opinions of the Tom-cat Murr," or, as we might say more briefly, *Tom Murr,* is a capital satire on German student life. The German scholar—there is, as far as I know, no English translation of the work—may there see how "Tommy" becomes a *Flotter Katzbursch.*

BOOK XIII.

CARBONARI.

Ma tua pianta radice non pone
Che su' pezzi d' infrante corone;
Nè si pasce di fresche ruggiade,
Ma di sangue di membra di re.

MONTI.

(*Motto of Constitution of the Eastern Lucanian Republic.*)

Translation.—Thy plant shall strike its roots only amidst the fragments of shattered crowns; no fresh dews shall nourish thee, but only the blood of regal limbs.

AUTHORITIES.

Memoirs of the Secret Societies of the South of Italy, particularly the Carbonari. London, 1821.

Saint-Edme. Constitution des Carbonari. Paris, 1821.

De Witt. Les Sociétés secrètes de France et d'Italie. Paris, 1830.

Orloff. Mémoires sur le royaume de Naples.

Colletta. Storia del reame di Napoli.

Le Blanc. L'Histoire de Dix Ans.

Gros. De Didier et autres conspirateurs sous la Restauration. Paris, 1841.

THE CARBONARI.

348.

HISTORY of the Association.—Like all other associations, the Carbonari lay claim to a very high antiquity. Some of the less instructed have even professed a descent from Philip of Macedon, the father of Alexander the Great, and have attempted to form a high degree founded on this imaginary origin. Others go back only so far as the pontificate of Alexander III., when Germany, to secure herself against rapacious barons, founded guilds and societies for mutual protection, and the charcoal-burners in the vast forests of that country united themselves against robbers and enemies. By words and signs only known to themselves, they afforded each other assistance. The criminal enterprise of Conrad de Kauffungen, to carry off the Saxon princes, failed through the intervention of the charcoal-burners. And at a period much more recent, the Duke Ulrich

of Würtemberg was compelled by them, under threat
of death, to abolish certain forest laws, considered
as oppressive. Similar societies arose in many
mountainous countries, and they surrounded themselves with that mysticism of which we have seen
so many examples. Their fidelity to each other
and to the society was so great, that it became in
Italy a proverbial expression to say, " On the faith
of a Carbonaro." But the most probable origin
of the order is to be found in that of the Hewers
(*Fendeurs*), which from very ancient times existed in the French department of the Jura,
where it was called *le bon cousinage* (the good
cousinship), and had rites similar to those of the
more modern Carbonari. The sect evidently spread
into Italy, where it acquired greater power and a
more perfect organization, and its members assumed
the new name of Carbonari. At the feasts of the
Carbonari, the Grand Master drinks to the health
of Francis I., King of France, the pretended
founder of the order, according to the following
tradition:—During the troubles in Scotland in Queen
Isabella's time—this Isabella is purely mythical—
many illustrious persons, having escaped from the
yoke of tyranny, took refuge in the woods. In
order to avoid all suspicion of criminal association,
they employed themselves in cutting wood and
making charcoal. Under pretence of carrying it
for sale, they introduced themselves into the vil-

lages, and bearing the name of real Carbonari
(colliers), they easily met their partisans, and
mutually communicated their different plans. They
recognized each other by signs, by touch and by
words, and as there were no habitations in the
forest, they constructed huts of an oblong form,
with branches of trees. Their lodges (*vendite*)
were subdivided into a number of baracche, each
erected by a Good Cousin of some distinction.
There dwelt in the forest a hermit of the name of
Theobald (349); he joined them and favoured their
enterprise. He was proclaimed protector of the
Carbonari. Now it happened that Francis I., King
of France, hunting on the frontiers of his kingdom
next to Scotland (*sic*), or following a wild beast,
was parted from his courtiers. He lost himself in
the forest, but stumbling on one of the baracche,
he was hospitably entertained, and eventually made
acquainted with their secret and initiated into the
order. On his return to France he declared himself its protector. The origin of this story is
probably to be found in the protection granted by
Louis XII. and continued by Francis I. to the
Waldenses, who had taken refuge in Dauphiné.
But neither the Hewers nor the Carbonari ever rose
to any importance, or acted any conspicuous part
among the secret societies of Europe till the period
of the Revolution. As to their influence in and
after that event, we shall return to it anon.

349. *St. Theobald.*—The Theobald alluded to in the foregoing tradition, is said to have been descended from the first Counts of Brie and Champagne.   Possessed of rank and wealth, his fondness for solitude led him to leave his father's house, and retire with his friend Gautier to a forest in Suabia, where they lived as hermits, working at any chance occupation by which they could maintain themselves, but chiefly by preparing charcoal for the forges.   They afterwards made several pilgrimages to holy shrines, and finally settled near Vicenza, where Gautier died.   Theobald died in 1066, and was canonized by Pope Alexander III.   From his occupation, St. Theobald was adopted as the patron saint of the Carbonari, and is invoked by the Good Cousins in their hymns; and a picture, representing him seated in front of his hut, is usually hung up in the lodge.

350. *The Vendita or Lodge.*—From the " Code of Carbonarism " we derive the following particulars respecting the lodge.   It is a room of wood in the shape of a barn.   The pavement must be of brick, the interior furnished with seats without backs.   At the end there must be a block supported by three legs, on which sits the Grand Master; at the two sides there must be two other blocks of the same size, on which sit the orator and secretary respectively.   On the block of the Grand Master there must be the following symbols: a

linen cloth, water, salt, a cross, leaves, sticks, fire, earth, a crown of white thorns, a ladder, a ball of thread, and three ribbons, one blue, one red, and one black. There must be an illuminated triangle with the initial letters of the pass-word of the second rank in the middle. On the left hand there must be a triangle, with the arms of the Vendita painted. On the right three transparent triangles, each with the initial letters of the sacred words of the first rank. The Grand Master, and first and second assistants, who also sit each before a large wooden block, hold hatchets in their hands. The masters sit along the wall of one side of the lodge, the apprentices opposite.

351. *Ritual of Initiation.*—The ritual of Carbonarism, as it was reconstituted at the beginning of the present century, was as follows. In the Initiation :—

"The Grand Master having opened the lodge, says, First Assistant, where is the first degree conferred ?

A. In the hut of a Good Cousin, in the lodge of the Carbonari.

G. M. How is the first degree conferred ?

A. A cloth is stretched over a block of wood, on which are arranged the bases, firstly, the cloth itself, water, fire, salt, the crucifix, a dry sprig, a green sprig. At least three Good Cousins must be present for an initiation ; the introducer, always

accompanied by a master, who remain outside the place where are the bases and the Good Cousins. The master who accompanies the introducer, strikes three times with his foot and cries : ' Masters, Good Cousins, I need succour.' The Good Cousins stand around the block of wood, against which they strike the cords they wear round the waist and make the sign, carrying the right hand from the left shoulder to the right side, and one of them exclaims, 'I have heard the voice of a Good Cousin who needs help, perhaps he brings wood to feed the furnaces.' The introducer is then brought in. Here the Assistant is silent, and the Grand Master begins again, addressing the new comer :—
' My Good Cousin, whence come you?

I. From the wood.

G. M. Whither go you?

I. Into the Chamber of Honour, to conquer my passions, submit my will, and be instructed in Carbonarism.

G. M. What have you brought from the wood?

I. Wood, leaves, earth.

G. M. Do you bring anything else?

I. Yes ; faith, hope, and charity.

G. M. Who is he whom you bring hither?

I. A man lost in the wood.

G. M. What does he seek?

I. To enter our order.

G. M. Introduce him.'

The neophyte is then brought in. The Grand Master puts several questions to him regarding his morals and religion, and then bids him kneel, holding the crucifix, and pronounce the oath :—' I promise and bind myself on my honour not to reveal the secrets of the Good Cousins; not to attack the virtue of their wives or daughters, and to afford all the help in my power to every Good Cousin needing it. So help me God ! '"

352. *First Degree.*—After some preliminary questioning the Grand Master addresses the novice thus: "What means the block of wood ?

N. Heaven and the roundness of the earth.

G. M. What means the cloth ?

N. That which hides itself on being born.

G. M. The water ?

N. That which serves to wash and purify from original sin.

G. M. The fire ?

N. To show us our highest duties.

G. M. The salt ?

N. That we are Christians.

G. M. The crucifix ?

N. It reminds us of our redemption.

G. M. What does the thread commemorate ?

N. The Mother of God that spun it.

G. M. What means the crown of white thorns ?

N. The troubles and struggles of Good Cousins.

G. M. What is the furnace ?

N. The school of Good Cousins.

G. M. What means the tree with its roots up in the air?

N. If all the trees were like that, the work of the Good Cousins would not be needed."

The catechism is much longer, but I have given only so much as will suffice to show the kind of instruction imparted in the first degree. Without any explanations following, one would think one was reading the catechism of one of those religions improvised on American soil, which seek by the singularity of form to stir up the imagination. But as in other societies, as that of the Illuminati, the object was not at the first onset to alarm the affiliated; his disposition had first to be tested before the real meaning of the ritual was revealed to him. Still some of the figures betray themselves, though studiously concealed. The furnace is the collective work at which the Carbonari labour; the sacred fire they keep alive, is the flame of liberty, with which they desire to illumine the world. They did not without design choose coal for their symbol; for coal is the fountain of light and warmth, that purifies the air. The forest represents Italy, the wild wood of Dante, infested with wild beasts, that is, foreign oppressors. The tree with the roots in the air is a figure of kingdoms destroyed and thrones overthrown. Catholic mysticism constantly re-appears, the highest honours are given to Christ, who was indeed the Good Cousin of all men. Carbonarism did not openly assail religious belief, but made use of it, endeavouring to simplify and reduce it to first principles, as Freemasonry does. The candidate, as in the last-named order, was supposed to perform journeys through the forest and through fire, to each of which a symbolical meaning was attached; though the true meaning was not told in this degree. In fact, to all who wished to gain an insight into the real objects of Carbonarism, this degree could not suffice. It was necessary to proceed.

353. *The Second Degree.*—The martyrdom of Christ occupies nearly the whole of the second degree, imparting to the catechism a sad character, calculated to surprise and terrify the candidate. The preceding figures were here invested with new and unexpected meanings, relating to the minutest particulars of the crucifixion of the Good Cousin Jesus; which more and more led the initiated to believe that the unusual and whimsical forms with stupendous artifice served to confound the ideas and suspicions of their enemies, and cause them to lose the traces of the fundamental idea. In the constant recurrence to the martyrdom of Christ we may discern two aims—the one essentially educational, to familiarize the Cousin with the idea of sacrifice, even, if necessary, of that of life; the other, chiefly political, intended to gain proselytes among the superstitious, the mystics, the souls loving Christi-

anity, fundamentally good, however prejudiced, because loving, and who constituted the greater number in a Roman Catholic country like Italy—then even more than now. The catechism, as already observed, has reference to the Crucifixion, and the symbols are all explained as representing something pertaining thereto. Thus the furnace signifies the Holy Sepulchre; the rustling of the leaves symbolizes the flagellation of the Good Cousin the Grand Master of the universe; and so on. The candidate for initiation into this degree has to undergo further trials. He represents Christ, whilst the Grand Master takes the name of Pilate, the first councillor that of Caiaphas, the second that of Herod; the Good Cousins generally are called the people. The candidate is led bound from one officer to the other, and finally condemned to be crucified; but he is pardoned on taking a second oath, more binding than the first, consenting to have his body cut in pieces and burnt, as in the former degree. But still the true secret of the order is not revealed.

354. *The Degree of Grand Elect.*—This degree is only to be conferred with the greatest precautions, secretly, and to Carbonari known for their prudence, zeal, courage, and devotion to the order. Besides, the candidates, who shall be introduced into a grotto of reception, must be true friends of the liberty of the people and ready to fight against tyrannical governments, who are the abhorred rulers of ancient

and beautiful Ausonia. The admission of the candidate takes place by voting, and three black balls are sufficient for his rejection. He must be thirty-three years and three months old, the age of Christ on the day of his death. But the religious drama is now followed by one political. The lodge is held in a remote and secret place, only known to the Grand Masters already received into the degree of Grand Elect. The lodge is triangular, truncated at the eastern end. The Grand Master Grand Elect is seated upon a throne. Two guards, from the shape of their swords called flames, are placed at the entrance. The assistants take the names of Sun and Moon respectively. Three lamps, in the shape of sun, moon, and stars are suspended at the three angles of the grotto or lodge. The catechism here reveals to the candidate that the object of the association is political, and aims at the overthrow of all tyrants, and the establishment of universal liberty, the time for which has arrived. To each prominent member his station and duties in the coming conflict are assigned, and the ceremony is concluded by all present kneeling down and pointing their swords to their breasts, whilst the Grand Elect pronounces the following formula:—"I, a free citizen of Ausonia, swear before the Grand Master of the Universe, and the Grand Elect Good Cousin, to devote my whole life to the triumph of the principles of liberty, equality, and progress, which are the soul of all the

secret and public acts of Carbonarism.   I promise
that, if it be impossible to restore the reign of liberty
without a struggle, I will fight to the death.   I consent, should I prove false to my oath, to be slain by
my Good Cousins Grand Elects ; to be fastened to
the cross in a lodge, naked, crowned with thorns ;
to have my belly torn open, the entrails and heart
taken out and scattered to the winds.   Such are
our conditions ; swear ! " The Good Cousins reply :
" We swear."   There was something theatrical in all
this ; but the organizers no doubt looked to the
effect it had on the minds of the initiated.   If on
this ground it could not be defended, then there is
little excuse for judicial wigs and clerical gowns,
episcopal gaiters and shovel-hats, lord mayors' shows,
parliamentary proceedings and royal pageants.

355. *Degree of Grand Master Grand Elect.*—
This, the highest degree of Carbonarism, is only
accessible to those who have given proofs of great
intelligence and resolution.   The Good Cousins
being assembled in the lodge, the candidate is
introduced blindfolded ; two members, representing
the two thieves, carry a cross, which is firmly
planted in the ground.   One of the two pretended
thieves is then addressed as a traitor to the cause,
and condemned to die on the cross.   He resigns himself to his fate, as fully deserved, and is tied to the
cross with silken cords ; and, to delude the candidate,
whose eyes are still bandaged, he utters loud groans.

The Grand Master pronounces the same doom on the other robber, but he, representing the non-repentant one, exclaims:—" I shall undergo my fate, cursing you, and consoling myself with the thought that I shall be avenged, and that strangers shall exterminate you to the last Carbonaro. Know that I have pointed out your retreat to the chiefs of the hostile army, and that within a short time you shall fall into their hands. Do your worst." The Grand Elect then turns to the candidate, and, alluding to the punishment awarded to traitors as done on the present occasion, informs him that he also must be fastened to the cross, if he persists in his intention to proceed, and there receive on his body the sacred marks, whereby the Grand Masters Grand Elects of all the lodges are known to each other, and must also pronounce the oath, whereupon the bandage will be removed, he will descend from the cross, and be clothed with the insignia of the Grand Master Grand Elect. He is then firmly tied to the cross, and pricked three times on the right arm, seven times on the left, and three times under the left breast. The cross being erected in the middle of the cave, that the members may see the marks on the body, on a given sign, the bandage being removed, the Cousins stand around the candidate, pointing their swords and daggers at his breast, and threatening him with even a worse death, should he turn traitor. They also watch his demeanour, and whether he betrays any fear. Seven toasts in his honour are then drunk, and the Grand Elect explains the real meaning of the symbols, which may not be printed, but is only to be written down, and zealously guarded, the owner promising to burn or swallow it, rather than let it fall into other hands. The Grand Master concludes by speaking in praise of the revolution already initiated, announcing its triumph not only in the peninsula, but everywhere where Italian is spoken, and exclaims:—" Very soon the nations weary of tyranny shall celebrate their victory over the tyrants; very soon" . . . Here the wicked thief exclaims:—"Very soon all ye shall perish !" Immediately there is heard outside the grotto the noise of weapons and fighting. One of the doorkeepers announces that the door is on the point of being broken open, and an assault on it is heard directly after. The Good Cousins rush to the door placed behind the crosses, and therefore unseen by the candidate ; the noise becomes louder, and there are heard the cries of Austrian soldiers; the Cousins return in great disorder, as if overpowered by superior numbers, say a few words of encouragement to the candidate fastened to the cross, and disappear through the floor, which opens beneath them. Cousins, dressed in the hated uniform of the foreigner, enter and marvel at the disappearance of the Carbonari. Perceiving the persons on the crosses, they, on finding them still alive, propose to kill them at once ; they charge and prepare to shoot them, when suddenly a number of balls fly into the cave, the soldiers fall down as if struck, and the Cousins re-enter through many openings, which at once close behind them, and shout :— "Victory! Death to tyranny! Long live the republic of Ausonia! Long live liberty! Long live the government established by the brave Carbonari!" In an instant the apparently dead soldiers and the two thieves are carried out of the cave ; and the candidate having been helped down from the cross, is proclaimed by the Grand Master, who strikes seven blows with his axe, a Grand Master Grand Elect.

356. *Signification of the Symbols.*—Not to interrupt the narrative, the explanation of the meaning of the symbols, given in this last degree, was omitted in the former paragraph, but follows here. It will be seen that it was not without reason that it was prohibited to print it. The cross serves to crucify the tyrant that persecutes us. The crown of thorns is to pierce his head. The thread denotes the cord to lead him to the gibbet, the ladder will aid him to mount. The leaves are nails to pierce his hands and feet. The pickaxe will penetrate his breast, and shed his impure blood. The axe will separate his head from his body. The salt will prevent the corruption of his head, that it

may last as a monument of the eternal infamy of despots. The pole will serve to put his head upon. The furnace will burn his body. The shovel will scatter his ashes to the wind. The baracca will serve to prepare new tortures for the tyrant, before he is slain. The water will purify us from the vile blood we shall have shed. The linen will wipe away our stains. The forest is the place where the Good Cousins labour to attain so important a result. These details are extracted from the minutes of the legal proceedings against the conspiracy of the Carbonari.

357. *Other Ceremonies and Regulations.*—The candidate having been received into the highest degree, other Good Cousins entered the cave, proclaiming the victory of the Carbonari and the establishment of the Ausonian republic; whereupon the lodge was closed. The members all bore pseudonyms, by which they were known in the order. These pseudonyms were entered in one book, whilst another contained their real names; and the two books were always kept concealed in separate places, so that the police, should they find one, should not be able to identify the conspirator. Officers of great importance were the Insinuators, Censors, Scrutators, and Coverers, whose appellations designate their duties. The higher officers were called Great Lights. Some of the affiliated, reserved for the most dangerous enterprises, were

styled the Forlorn Hope; others *Stabene,* or the
" Sedentary," who were not advanced beyond the
first degree, on account of want of intelligence or
courage.   Like the Freemasons, the Carbonari had
their own almanacs, dating their era from Francis I.
The ritual and the ceremonies, as partly detailed
above, were probably strictly followed on particularly important occasions only ; as to their origin,
little is known concerning it—most likely they were
invented among the Neapolitans.   Nor were they
always and at all places alike, but the spirit that
breathed in them was permanent and universal ;
and that it was the spirit of liberty and justice can
scarcely be denied, especially after the events of the
last decade.   The following summary of a manifesto
proceeding from the Society of the Carbonari will
show this very clearly.

358. *The Ausonian Republic.*—The epoch of the
following document, of which, however, an abstract
only is here given, is unknown.   The open proceedings of Carbonarism give us no clue, because in
many respects they deviate from the programme of
this sectarian charter; sectarian, inasmuch as the
document has all the fulness of a social pact.   But
to whatever time these statutes belong, they cannot
be read without the liveliest interest.

Italy, to which new times shall give a new name,
sonorous and pure, Ausonia (the ancient Latin name),
must be free from its threefold sea to the highest

summit of the Alps. The territory of the republic
shall be divided into twenty-one provinces, each of
which shall send a representative to the National
Assembly. Every province shall have its local
assembly; all citizens, rich or poor, may aspire to
all public charges; the mode of electing judges
is strictly laid down; two kings, severally elected
for twenty-one years, one of whom is to be called
the king of the land, the other of the sea, shall be
chosen by the sovereign assembly; all Ausonian
citizens are soldiers; all fortresses not required to
protect the country against foreigners shall be razed
to the ground; new ports are to be constructed
along the coasts, and the navy enlarged; Christianity shall be the State religion, but every other
creed shall be tolerated; the college of cardinals
may reside in the republic during the life of the
pope reigning at the time of the promulgation of
this charter—after his death, the college of cardinals
will be abolished; hereditary titles and feudal rights
are abolished; hospitals, charitable institutions, col-
leges, lyceums, primary and secondary schools, shall
be largely increased, and properly allocated; punishment of death is inflicted on murderers only,
transportation to one of the islands of the republic
being substituted for all other punishments; monastic institutions are preserved, but no man can become a monk before the age of forty-five, and no
woman a nun before that of forty, and even after

having pronounced their vows, they may re-enter their own families. Mendicity is not allowed; the country finds work for able paupers, and succour for invalids. The tombs of great men are placed along the highways; the honour of a statue is awarded by the sovereign assembly. The constitutional pact may be revised every twenty-one years.

359. *Other Charter.*—A charter or project, said to have been proposed by the Carbonari to the English Government in 1813, when the star of Napoleon was fast declining, is to the following effect:—Italy shall be free and independent. Its boundaries shall be the three seas and the Alps. Corsica, Sardinia, Sicily, the seven islands, and the islands along the coasts of the Mediterranean, Adriatic, and Ionian Seas shall form an integral portion of the Roman empire. Rome shall be the capital of the empire . . . As soon as the French shall have evacuated the peninsula, the new emperor shall be elected from among the reigning families of Naples, Piedmont, or England. Illyria shall form a kingdom of itself, and be given to the King of Naples as an indemnity for Sicily. This project in some respects widely differs from the one preceding it, and there is great doubt whether it ever emanated from the Carbonari.

360. *Carbonarism and Murat.*—The excessive number of the affiliated soon disquieted rulers, and especially Murat, King of Naples whose fears were increased by a letter from Dandolo, Councillor

of State, saying :—" Sire, Carbonarism is spreading in Italy; free your kingdom from it, if possible, because the sect is opposed to thrones." Maghella, a native of Genoa, who became Minister of Police under Murat, advised that king, on the other hand, to declare openly against Napoleon, and to proclaim the independence of Italy, and for that purpose to favour the Carbonari; but Murat was too irresolute to follow the course thus pointed out, and declared against the Carbonari. The measures taken by him, however, only increased the activity of the sect and the hopes of the banished Bourbons, who in the neighbouring Sicily watched every turn of affairs that might promise their restoration. Murat proscribed the sect, which induced it to seek the assistance of England, as we have already seen (359). It also grew into favour with the Bourbons and Lord William Bentinck. The emissaries sent to Palermo, to come to terms with the exiled royal family, returned to Naples with a plan fully arranged, the results of which were soon seen in Calabria and the Abruzzi. The promise of a constitution was the lure with which England—whose chief object, however, was the overthrow of Napoleon—attracted the sectaries; the Bourbons, constrained by England, promised the Neapolitans a liberal constitution on their being restored to the throne. The Prince of Moliterno suggested to England that the only means of defeating France was to favour Italian unity; and the idea was soon widely promulgated and advocated throughout the country. Murat sent General Manhès against the Carbonari, with orders to exterminate them. Many of the leaders were captured and executed, but the sect nevertheless succeeded in effecting a partial and temporary revolution in favour of the Bourbons; which, however, was soon quelled by the energetic measures of Queen Caroline Murat, who was regent during her husband's then absence. About this time, also, dissensions arose among the members of the sect; its leaders, seeing the difficulty of directing the movements of so great a confederacy, conceived the plan of a reform, and executed it with secrecy and promptitude. The members who were retained continued to bear the name of Carbonari, while those who were expelled, according to some accounts, took that of Calderari (Braziers), and an implacable hatred arose between the rival sects. Murat wavered for some time between the two parties, and at last determined on supporting the Carbonari, who were most numerous. But it was too late. They had no confidence in him; and they also knew his desperate circumstances. Murat fell.

361. *Carbonarism and the Bourbons.*—The fall of Joachim pleased the Carbonari, as that of Napoleon was grateful to the Freemasons; but the latter did not suffer by the restoration, though the former did. King Ferdinand secretly disliked the sect, and only

thought of kicking down the ladder by which he had reascended the throne. He refused to keep the promises he had made, and forbade the holding of Carbonari meetings. The Prince of Canova, who became Minister of Police in 1819, determined to exterminate them. For this purpose he formed the Brigands, who had played a part in the sanguinary scenes of 1799, into a new society, of which he himself became the head, inviting all the old Calderari to join him, on account of their enmity to the Carbonari. He required them to take the following oath:—"I, A. B., promise and swear upon the Trinity, upon this cross and upon this steel, the avenging instrument of the perjured, to live and die in the Roman Catholic and Apostolic faith, and to defend with my blood this religion and the society of True Friendship, the Calderari. I swear never to offend, in honour, life, or property, the children of True Friendship, &c. I swear eternal hatred to all Masonry, and its atrocious protectors, as well as to all Jansenists, Materialists (Molinists?), Economists, and Illuminati. I swear, that if through wickedness or levity I suffer myself to be perjured, I submit to the loss of life, and then to be burnt, &c." But the king having learnt what his minister had been attempting without his knowledge, deprived him of his office and banished him; and thus his efforts came to nothing. In 1819 took place the rising at Cadiz, by which the King of Spain, Ferdinand VII., was compelled to give Spain constitutional privileges. This again stirred up the Carbonari; but there was no unanimity in their counsels, and their intrigues only led to many being imprisoned and others banished. An attempt made in 1820 extorted a constitution; the leader was the Abbé Menichini. The influence of the Carbonari increased; lodges were established everywhere. Even the women now began to become connected with the sect; and female lodges with the title of "the Garden Women" (*le Giardiniere*) were formed, each sister taking the name of a flower. The secrets of Carbonarism, its signs, words, and symbols were openly proclaimed, and blessed in the churches. But the triumph of Carbonarism did not last long. Austrian influence, the disloyalty of the king, and treason in the sect itself, put an end to it in 1821.

362. *Carbonarism and the Church.*—The Carbonari in the Roman States aimed at the overthrow of the papal power, and chose the moment when the pope was expected to die to carry out their scheme. They had collected large forces and provisions at Macerata; but the sudden recovery of the pope put a stop to the enterprise. The leaders were betrayed into the hands of the government, and some of them condemned to death and others to perpetual imprisonment; though the pope afterwards commuted the sentences. The sect of the

Sanfedisti (391) was founded to counteract the efforts of the Carbonari.

363. *Carbonarism in Northern Italy.*—In Lombardy and Venetia also the Carbonari had their lodges, and their object was the expulsion of the foreigner, the Austrian. But here also they failed; and among the victims of the failure were Silvio Pellico, Confalonieri, Castiglia, Torelli, Maroncelli, and many others, who, after having been exposed on the pillory at Milan and other places, were sent to Spielberg and other German fortresses.

364. *Carbonarism in France.*—Carbonarism was introduced into France by Joubert and Dugier, who had taken part in revolutionary movements in their own country in 1820, and after having for some time taken refuge in Italy, where they had joined the Carbonari, brought their principles to France, on their return from their expatriation. The sect made rapid progress among the French; all the students at the different universities became members. Lafayette was chosen its chief. Lodges existed at La Rochelle, Poitiers, Niort, Bordeaux, Colmar, Neuf-Brisach, and Belfort, where in 1821 an unsuccessful attempt was made against the government. Risings in other places equally failed; and though the society still continued to exist, and had a share in the events of the revolution of 1830, still, considering the number of its members and the great resources and influence it consequently pos-

sessed, it cannot be said to have produced any adequate results. It marks, however, a transition period in the history of secret societies. From secret societies occupied with religion, philosophy, and politics in the abstract, it leads us to the secret societies whose objects are more immediately and practically political. And thus in France, Italy, and other states, it gave rise to numerous and various sects, wherein we find the men of thought and those of action combining for one common object—the progress, as they understood it, of human society. Carbonarism, in fact, was revived about the year 1825, and some ten years after combined, or rather coalesced, with the society known as Young Italy, whose aims were identical with those of the Carbonari—the expulsion of the foreigner from Italian soil, and the unification of Italy. The Carbonari succeeded, in 1831, in driving the Duchess of Parma, Maria Louisa, into exile. One of her most trusted councillors was a Carbonaro, who, when she entered her carriage, coolly wished her a happy journey, to which she replied by saying to the lady of honour that accompanied her, " What a Judas ! " The triumph of the Carbonari however lasted only twenty-eight days; the duchess at the end of that period re-entered her capital, Austria having by force of arms effected her restoration.

BOOK XIV.

THE INQUISITION.

THE INQUISITION.

365.

INTRODUCTORY.—The earth in the Colosseum at Rome is said to be soaked with the blood of Christian martyrs. Some pope—I forget which—to convince a heretic, is reported to have taken up a handful of the earth, squeezed it, and caused drops of blood to fall from it. Supposing, for argument's sake, the legend, and the assertion on which it is founded, to be true, the Christian Church has well avenged her martyrs. To accomplish her ends, the Romish Church established the Inquisition.

366. *Establishment of Institution.*—Innocent III. established it in 1208 in Languedoc. Peter of Castelnau having been sent to preach against the heretics, he was slain by the Albigenses. As soon as his death became known he was canonized, and the fourth Council of the Lateran, at the instigation of the pope, sanctioned and organized the Inquisi-

tion, the original idea of which was due to Dominique de Guzman, who also founded the order of Dominican friars.   The Council, or rather the pope, decreed that all heretics should be delivered over to the secular arm, and their property confiscated.   Sovereigns were called upon to drive all heretics from their states; in case of non-obedience, the pope would offer their territory to whosoever could conquer them.   Persons who had favoured heretics, or received them into their houses, were to be excommunicated and declared infamous, incapable of inheriting property, and not entitled to Christian burial.   Guzman, rightly considering that the foul band of preaching friars, whom he had associated with himself, were not the sort of people to further his views—for those men were too fanatical, not to be violent, which would have been injurious to the new institution, further organized his " Militia of Christ," a religious police, composed of bigoted men and women, belonging to all classes of society, even to the highest; of criminals, as we have seen in the account of the " Garduna;" of fools and knaves.   This invisible troop of spies and denouncers, these familiars of the Inquisition, as they afterwards called themselves, formed the *secret* portion of the Inquisition, and were none the less formidable on that account.   From 1233, when the Inquisition was established in Spain, to the beginning of the next century, it made rapid

progress, spreading into Italy and Germany. In
1308 the Inquisition persecuted the Templars *à
outrance; autos-da-fe,* " acts of faith," as the burning of heretics was called, shed their lurid light
over many a Spanish city, at which the royal family
frequently were present.

367. *Progress of Institution.*—Until the joint
reign of Ferdinand and Isabella, the Inquisition
in Spain had been confined to the kingdom of Aragon. But about 1481 the queen established it in
Castille, and the king gradually extended its jurisdiction over all his states. Like James of Scotland,
the King of Spain always wanted "siller;" the
Inquisition offered him a third of all the property it
confiscated, and promised him a large share of the
riches of the thousands of Jews then living in Spain;
the nobles of Aragon and Castille were always conspiring against him, the Inquisition would quietly
and secretly get hold of their persons, and thus rid
him of these enemies; heaven was to be gained by
putting down heresy; here surely were reasons
enough for protecting the Inquisition and investing
it with full powers. The queen also—alas, that it
has to be said of her!—was greatly in favour of it,
and even requested the pope to declare the sentences pronounced in Spain to be final and without
appeal to Rome. She complained at the same time
that the people accused her of having no other view
in establishing the Inquisition than that of sharing

with its officers the property of those condemned by them. The pope, Sixtus IV., granted everything, and appeased her conscientious scruples as to confiscations. A bull, dated 1483, named father Thomas de Torquemada, an atrocious fanatic, Grand Inquisitor of Spain. For eighteen years he held the office, condemning on the average ten thousand victims annually to death by fire, starvation, torture. In the first six months of his sanguinary rule 298 *marranos*—Moors or Jews, that had been converted to Christianity—were burnt at the stake in Seville alone, and 70 condemned to imprisonment for life. During the same space of time, 2,000 *marranos* were burnt alive in various other places; a greater number, who had been fortunate enough to make their escape before they were seized—for when once in the power of the terrible tribunal there was little chance of evasion—were burnt in effigy; and about 17,000 persons, accused on the charge of heresy, underwent various other punishments. Upwards of 20,000 victims in half a year! Torquemada was so abhorred that he never stirred abroad without being surrounded by 250 familiars, and on his table always lay a horn of the unicorn, which was supposed to possess the virtue of discovering and nullifying the force of poison. His cruelties excited so many complaints that the pope himself was startled, and three times Torquemada was obliged to justify his conduct.

368. *Judicial Procedure of the Inquisition.*— Before proceeding with our historical details, let us briefly state the mode of procedure adopted by the execrable tribunal of the Inquisition.

A denunciation, verbal or in writing, and it little mattered from what impure source it proceeded, formed the starting point. Every year, on the third Sunday in Lent, the " Edict of Denunciation" was read in the churches, enjoining every person, on pain of major excommunication, to reveal within six days to the Holy Office, as the Inquisition was now styled, facts opposed to the purity of faith, that might have come to their notice. The most trifling acts exposed persons to the charge of heresy ; to put a clean cloth on the table on a Saturday, the Jewish Sabbath, smelled of Judaism ; to put on clean linen on a Friday, the Mahometan Sunday, betrayed Mahometanism. The opinions of Luther, casting horoscopes, eating with Jews, dining or supping with friends on the eve of a journey, as the Jews do, these and a hundred other things equally innocent, might lead to the stake !

After having drawn up a lying act of accusation, based on the statements of a vile or revengeful informer, the intended victim was pounced upon by the alguazils of the Santa Hermandad, or holy brotherhood. His property was put under sequestration, and the claw of the Holy Office was one that seldom released its prey. He was then carried to a special dungeon, called the *casa santa,* generally underground, that the cries of the prisoners might not be heard—a dark and noisome cell, which, when the Holy Office had many victims, he had to share with other prisoners, with no accommodation for decency or necessity, full of poisonous effluvia, with nothing to lie upon but putrid straw; this became his abode, to which no one ever gained access, except his jailors. Sometimes he was left to die of starvation, or kept for years in this prison, whilst no one dared raise a voice in his behalf. People disappeared, and their relations and friends only surmised, and cautiously whispered among themselves their suspicions that they were languishing, or had perhaps already died, in the dungeons of the Inquisition. Carlyle has somewhere said: "There are twenty-eight millions of inhabitants in England, mostly fools;" but does not this apply with much greater force to a people that could for centuries submit to such tyranny as the Spaniards and other nations did? When the prisoner was at last brought before his judges, he was exhorted to confess his crime, but he was not informed of the charge against him; and if he did not know what to confess, or if his confession did not agree with the secret information against him, he was taken to the torture chamber to extort what was wanted. As the inquisitors were profoundly religious men, (!) regulating their conduct by the teaching of Christ, which forbids the shedding of blood, they had with hellish ingenuity contrived their instruments of torture, so that they should avoid that result, and yet inflict the greatest suffering the human body can possibly bear, without having the vital spark extinguished in it. It is true that the pendulum torture —which certainly was applied—as the instrument was discovered as late as the year 1820, in the prison of the Inquisition at Seville—proved that the rule was broken through; but the modern Inquisitors, it appears, were not so conscientious as the ancient !

369. *Tortures.*—There were three modes of torture chiefly in use. The first was that of the cord. The prisoner's arms were tied behind him with one end of a long rope, which passed over a pulley fixed in the vault of the chamber; he was then raised from the ground to a considerable height, which, by twisting his arms backward and above his head, was sufficient to dislocate the shoulder joints; the rope was then suddenly slackened, so that he fell to within a foot or so from the ground, by which his arms were nearly torn out of their sockets, and his whole body sustained a fearful concussion. In some cases the back of the victim, in being drawn up, was made to press against a roller, set round with sharp spikes, causing of course fearful laceration. Another mode of applying the cord torture was by fastening the victim down on a sort of wooden bed,

and encircling his arms and legs in different places with thin cord, which by means of winches could be so tightened as to cut deep into the flesh. If these tortures found the prisoner firm, and extorted no confession, it was generally in the above position that he was subjected to the torture by water. His mouth and nostrils were covered with a thick cloth, and one of the Satanic brood of Dominican friars would sit by him, and through a funnel pour water on the cloth, which speedily became soaked, and then more water being poured on, the latter would enter the mouth of the unfortunate wretch lying there in fearful agony, undergoing all the pangs of slow suffocation, while his brow was covered with the cold sweat of death, and the blood started from his eyes and nostrils; and all the time the fiend by his side exhorted him, "for the love of Him who died on the Cross," to confess. The third mode of torture was by fire. The victim was stretched and fastened on the ground; the soles of his feet were exposed and rubbed with oil or lard, or any other easily inflammable matter, and then a portable fire was placed against them; the intense torture the burning of the greasy matter spread on the soles caused to the unfortunate prisoner, may be imagined. When, in consequence of it, the prisoner declared himself ready to confess, a screen was interposed between his feet and the fire; on its withdrawal, if the confession was not satisfactory, the pain was even more frightful than before. The wretches who, at the Inquisitor's command, executed all these terrible operations on their fellow-creatures, wore long black gowns with hoods, covering their heads, having holes for mouth, nostrils, and eyes.

Another diabolical device of the Inquisitors consisted in this, that while they asserted that the torture or being put to the question could only be applied once, they declared the torture *suspended*, when it was found that by continuing it at the time the victim would die under their hands, and thus deprive them of the further gratification of their thirst for cruelty. The torture was begun, but not finished, and the unfortunate wretch could thus be put to the question as often as they pleased, the torture was only being *continued !* The Inquisitors further were the first to put women to the torture; neither the weakness nor the modesty of the sex had any influence on them. The Dominican friars would flog naked women in the corridors of the Inquisition building, after having first violated them, for some slight breach of discipline! Even after this lapse of time, it makes one's blood boil with indignation when thinking of those horrors !

370. *Condemnation and Execution of Prisoners.*— Out of every two thousand persons accused, perhaps one escaped condemnation to death or life-long imprisonment. The most fortunate—those that were *reconciled*—had to appear, bareheaded, with a

cord round their neck; clothed in the *san benito*, an ugly garment, something like a sack, with black and yellow or white stripes, and carrying a green wax taper in their hands, in the hall of the tribunal, or sometimes openly in a church, where, on their knees, they abjured the heresies laid to their charge. They were then condemned to wear the ignominious garment for some considerable time.   Several other degrading and troublesome conditions were imposed on them, and the greater portion or whole of their property was confiscated ; this was a rule the holy fathers never departed from.   The *relaxed*, or those condemned to death, dressed in an even more hideous garb than the " reconciled," having the portrait of the victim immersed in flames, and devils dancing round about it painted thereon, were led out to the place of execution, attended by monks and friars, and burnt at the stake, the court, Grand Inquisitor, his officers, and the people witnessing the agonies of the dying, and inhaling the flavour of their burning flesh with intense satisfaction.   One trait of mercy the monkish demons showed consisted in first strangling those that died penitent before burning them, whilst those who maintained their innocence to the last were burnt alive.   These bloody recreations at last became so fashionable, that in Spain and Portugal the accession of a king, a royal marriage, or the birth of a prince, were celebrated by a grand *auto-da-fe*, for which as many victims were reserved or procured as possible.

371. *History continued.*—The monster Torquemada was still Inquisitor-General. The people of Aragon, who had from the first violently opposed the establishment of the Inquisition in their territory, were exasperated when *autos-da-fe* began to be celebrated among them, and in order to intimidate their butchers slew the most violent of their oppressors, one Peter Arbuès of Epila, at the altar. The church immediately placed him among her martyrs, Queen Isabella erected a statue to him; his body wrought miracles, and the present pope, Pius IX., has canonized him. The just death of the Inquisitor of course led to increased cruelty and persecution on the part of the Holy Office; the men who slew Arbuès unfortunately were captured; they had their hands cut off before being hanged, and their bodies were cut up in pieces, which were exposed on the highways. Torquemada next urged on the king and queen to expel the Jews from their states, as enemies of the Christian religion. The Jews, informed of their danger, offered the king thirty thousand ducats towards the expenses of the war with Granada, on condition that they were allowed to stay. Ferdinand and Isabella were on the point of acceding to this proposal, when Torquemada, a crucifix in his hand, presented himself to the sovereigns, and thus

addressed them: " Judas was the first to sell his master for thirty pieces of silver. Your highnesses intend selling him a second time for thirty thousand pieces of gold. Here he is, take him, and speedily conclude the sale!" Of course the proud king and equally haughty queen cringed before the insolent friar, and the decree went forth on the 31st March, 1492, that by the 31st July of the same year all Jews must have quitted the states of Ferdinand and Isabella, on pain of death and confiscation of all their property. Some 800,000 Jews emigrated, momentarily saving their lives, but scarcely any property, since the time was too short for realising it at its value. Thousands of men, women, and children, perished by the way, so that the Jews compared their sufferings to those their forefathers underwent at the time of Titus. When, shortly after this expulsion of the Jews, the kingdom of Granada was conquered by the Spanish arms, the conquest was considered as heaven's special approval and reward; and Ferdinand, to show his religious zeal, committed every kind of cruelty his soul could invent. After the capture of Malaga, twelve Jews, who had taken refuge there, underwent by his direct orders the terrible death by pointed reeds, a slow but fatal torture, like being stabbed to death with pins.

Torquemada died in 1498; his successor, the Dominican Deza, introduced the Inquisition into the newly conquered kingdom of Granada ; 80,000 Moors, preferring exile to baptism, left the country. He also introduced the terrible tribunal into Naples and Sicily, and though the Sicilians at first rose against it, and expelled the Inquisitors, they had afterwards, overcome by Charles V., to submit to its re-establishment. Deza, during his short reign of nine years, caused 2,592 individuals to be burnt alive and 829 in effigy, and condemned upwards of 32,000 to imprisonment and the galleys, with total confiscation of property. He was succeeded by the mild Ximenés, after whom came Adrien Boeijens, who was as cruel a persecutor as Torquemada; the Lutheran doctrines, now gaining ground, gave him and his successors plenty of occupation, and the bonfires of the Inquisition blazed not only in Spain, but at Naples, Malta, Venice, in Sardinia and Flanders; and in the Spanish colonies in America the poor Indians perished in hecatombs, for either refusing to be baptized, or being suspected of having relapsed into their former idolatry, after having adopted and professed the mild and gentle creed of Christianity.

372. *The False Nuncio.*—The Inquisition was introduced into Portugal in a manner worthy of that tribunal. In 1539 there appeared at Lisbon a papal legate, who declared to have come to Portugal, there to re-establish the Inquisition. He brought the king letters from Pope Paul III.,

and produced the most ample credentials for nominating a Grand Inquisitor and all other officers of the sacred tribunal. This man was a clever swindler, called John Perés, of Saavedra, who was an adept at imitating all kinds of writing and forging signatures and seals. He was attended by a magnificent train of more than a hundred servants, and to defray his expenses had borrowed at Seville enormous sums in the name of the Apostolic Chamber at Rome. The king was at first surprised and angry that the pope should send an envoy of this description without previous notice; but Perés haughtily replied that in so urgent a matter as the establishment of the Inquisition and the suppression of heresy the Holy Father could not stand on points, and that the king was highly honoured by the fact that the first messenger who brought him the news was the legate himself. The king dared complain no more; and the false nuncio the same day nominated a Grand Inquisitor, set up the Holy Office, and collected money for its working expenses; before news could come from Rome, the rogue had already pocketed upwards of two hundred thousand ducats. But he could not make his escape before the swindle was discovered, and Perés was condemned to be whipped and sent to the galleys for ten years. But the best of the joke was that the pope confirmed all the swindler had done; in the plentitude of his divine power, Paul III. declared

the slight irregularities that attended the establishment of the Portuguese Inquisition not to affect its
jurisdiction or moral character, and that now it was
established, it should remain so.

373. *General History of Institution continued.*—
We need not go through the list of Grand Inquisitors *seriatim.* Let us only give particular
facts, indicative of the spirit that continued to guide
them. Under the generalate of Valdés, the eighth
Inquisitor-General, an old lady, Marie de Bour-
gogne, immensely rich, was denounced by a
servant as having said : " Christians respect neither
faith nor law." She was thereupon cast into one
of the dungeons of the Holy Office, where she
remained for five years, for want of proof. At the
end of that time she was put to the torture, to
extort an avowal, and she was so unmercifully
racked, that she died under the butchers' hands.
She was then ninety years of age. But her trial
was continued after her death, and ended in her
remains being condemned to be burnt, and the total
confiscation of her property; her children, besides
being disinherited, also being declared infamous
for ever.

Philip II. extended the jurisdiction of the Inquisition throughout the Netherlands, and in spite
of the resistance of the inhabitants, met with
such success, that his noble executioner, the Duke
of Alba, could boast of having within five years

sent to the stake and gallows eighteen thousand persons for the crime of heresy. But the oppression at last became so great, that the Netherlands revolted again, and this time successfully; they for ever threw off the Spanish yoke. It was during this Dutch war of liberation that the mysterious catastrophe of Don Carlos, Philip's son by his first wife, occurred. Romance asserts that the tragedy had its origin in the love passages said to have taken place between Don Carlos and Philip's second wife, Elizabeth of France, who before becoming his step-mother, had been his affianced bride. But history explains the facts in this way: Don Carlos conspired against his father, a gloomy tyrant, who deprived him of every scrap of power and influence, keeping him in the perfect subjection of a child; the prince thought of assassinating the king, or flying to the Netherlands, which he hoped to erect into an independent kingdom for himself. While he was hesitating, the Inquisition discovered both incipient schemes, revealed them to the king, and pronounced either deserving of death. Don Carlos was seized, imprisoned, and killed by poison. It is difficult to imagine a moral monster such as Philip II. was. He caused the works of Vésale, his own physician, who first taught the true facts and principles of anatomy, with their illustrations by Titian, to be publicly burnt, and the doctor himself was compelled to make an involuntary pilgrimage to Jerusalem to expiate his impious attempt of prying into the secrets of nature. This, we may say, was simply absurd on the part of the king; what follows is atrocious. In 1559 he learnt that an *auto-da-fe* had taken place in a distant locality, where thirty persons had perished at the stake. He besought the Inquisitors to be allowed to witness a similar spectacle; the Dominican devils, to encourage and reward such holy zeal on the part of heaven's anointed, sent out their archers, who searched with such diligence for victims, that on the 6th October of the same year, the king was able to preside at Valladolid at the burning of forty of his subjects, which gave him the most lively satisfaction. One of the condemned, a person of distinction, implored the royal mercy, as he was being led to the stake. " No," replied the crowned hyena, " if it were my own son I would surrender him to the flames, if he persisted in his heresy."

In 1566 the Grand Inquisitor Espinosa began his crusade against the Moors that still remained in Spain. For a long time the persecuted race confined themselves to remonstrances, but when it was decreed that their children must thenceforth be brought up in the Christian faith, a vast conspiracy was formed, which for nine months was kept secret, and would have been successful, had not the Moors of the mountainous districts broken out into open rebellion before those of the country and towns were prepared to support them. The Christians scattered among the Moorish population of course were the first victims of the long pent-up rage of the Mussulmans. Three thousand perished at the first outset ; all the monks of a monastery were cast into boiling oil. One of the insurgents, the intimate friend of a Christian, knew of no greater proof of affection he could show him, than transfixing him with his lance, lest others should treat him worse. The Marquis of Mondejar, captain-general of Andalusia, was appointed to put down the insurrection. As he was too humane, his reprisals not being severe enough, the Marquis de Los Velez, called by the Moors the " Demon with the Iron Head," was associated with him in the command, and he carried on war in the most ferocious manner. At the battle of Ohanez, blood was shed in such quantities, that the thirsty Spaniards could not find one unpolluted spring. One thousand six hundred Moors were subjected to a treatment worse than death, and immediately after Los Velez and his band of butchers celebrated the feast of the Purification of the Virgin ! And in the end the superior number of the Christians triumphed over Moorish bravery, and the Inquisitors were busy for weeks holding *autos-da-fe* to celebrate the victory of the true faith.

Under the long reign of Philip II., called the

"Demon of the South," six Grand Inquisitors carried on their bloody orgies. The reformed creed of course supplied the greatest numbers of victims; at Seville on one occasion eight hundred were arrested all at once. At the first *auto-da-fe* of Valladolid, on 12th May, 1559, fourteen members of one family were burnt. The Inquisition was established in the island of Sardinia, at Lima, Mexico, Cartagena, in the fleet, army, and even among custom-house officers.

Philip III. of Spain was early taught the power of the Inquisition. For when, at the beginning of his reign, he was obliged to be present at an *auto-da-fe*, and could not restrain his tears at seeing two young women, one Jewish and the other Moorish, burnt at the stake, for no other fault than that of having been brought up in the different creeds of their fathers, the Inquisitors imputed to him his compassion as a crime, which could only be expiated by blood; the king had to submit to being bled and seeing his blood burnt by the executioner.

Philip IV. inaugurated his reign by an *auto-da-fe*. The Inquisitor-General gave to the show of the *auto-da-fe*, whose interest began to decline, a new zest by causing the sentence of death against ten *marranos* to be read to them, while each of them had one hand nailed to a wooden cross.

The marriage of Charles II. with the niece of

Louis XIV. (1680) was celebrated with an *auto-da-fe* at Madrid, at which figured 118 victims, most of whom were burnt. Is it possible to realize the horrors of this transaction—a man brought up in the principles of chivalry and a woman of royal birth, whom one would suppose to be not only noble but also gentle, witnessing, on their wedding-day, when one would imagine their hearts to be full of joy and therefore full of good-will towards all men, and especially their subjects, so cruel a spectacle as the burning alive of human beings, burnt, so to say, in their honour? But here we see the effects of evil church government and priestly influence. When the mania of burning every old woman who had a black cat, as a witch, arose, the Inquisition found a new field of labour; and whatever might be the density of mental darkness with which priests and monks covered Europe, they took care there should be plenty of material light, and hence the funeral pyres of human reason and liberty were always blazing. Some of the Molinists, who, under pretext of " Perfect Contemplation," encouraged the most scandalous sexual excesses, were also burnt, not on account of their immoral practices, but because of some so-called heretical notions they propounded.

Under the succeeding kings of Spain general enlightenment and civilization had made too much progress to allow the Inquisitors to indulge as formerly their frantic rage and fanatical cruelty. During the reign of Ferdinand VI., Charles III., and Charles IV., they obtained only 245 condemnations, of which fourteen were to death. Freemasons and Jansenists were the principal victims.

On the 4th December, 1808, Napoleon suppressed the Inquisition, and its papers and documents were joyfully burnt at a last but liberating *auto-da-fe.* But Ferdinand VII., on his restoration in 1814, re-established the Inquisition, and appointed Francis Miéry Campilla, Bishop of Almeria, its forty-fifth and last Inquisitor-General. Immediately the prisons, galleys, and penal colonies were filled with prisoners. In 1820, however, all the Spanish provinces combined in a general insurrection, broke the bonds of absolutism, definitively crushed the Inquisition and its familiars, set free its prisoners, demolished its palaces and prisons, and burnt its instruments of torture. In the same way it was abolished in Portugal, and in the East and West Indies. It exists now only at Rome, having been restored by Pius VIII., but is reduced to a tribunal of clerical discipline. Its palace is still standing, but its dungeons are empty, and its upper rooms turned into barracks, except a few yet inhabited by some priests.

BOOK XV.

MINOR ITALIAN SECTS.

"*Mephistopheles* (*loq.*)—Away! Do not trouble me with these feuds of tyranny and slavery. I am weary of them, for when they are scarcely settled, they begin afresh; and none discern that it is only Asmodeus mocking them. They contend, they say, for rights of liberty; but closely examined, it's slaves against slaves."—*Faust.*

AUTHORITIES.

Carte segrete e atti ufficiali della polizia austriaca in Italia dal 4 Giugno 1814, al 22 Marzo 1848. Capolago, 1851.

Documenti della Guerra Santa d' Italia. 1850.

Storia delle Società Secrete. Di Perini. Milano, 1863.

L'Italie Rouge. Par le Vte D'Arlincourt. Paris, 1850.

Della Difesa di Venezia. Di F. Carrano. Geneva, 1850.

Histoire des Etats Italiens. Par le Vte de Beaumont-Vassy. Bruxelles, 1851.

Lionello, o delle Società Secrete. Napoli, 1863.

Le Società Secrete. Di V. Gioberti. Napoli, 1852.

I.

INDEPENDENTS.

374.

INSURRECTIONARY *Centres in Italy.*—In that vast net of conspiracies which once covered all Italy, it is difficult always to discern chief threads from secondary ones, or the connection between them. Though the elements of comparison abound, we miss those minute notices that historically establish the bonds between the various centres of activity. And the story of Italian movements is that of provincial risings, which only in course of time were fused into one single mass. The insurrections since 1848 were signs of the maturity of the time.

375. *Guelphic Knights.*—One of the most important societies that issued from the midst of the Carbonari was that of the Guelphic Knights, who were very powerful in all parts of Italy. A report of the Austrian police says :—" This society is the

most dangerous, on account of its origin and diffusion, and the profound mystery which surrounds it. It is said that this society derives its origin from England or Germany." Its origin, nevertheless, was purely Italian. The councils consisted of six members, who, however, did not know each other, but intercommunicated by means of one person, called the "Visible," because he alone was visible. Every council also had one youth of undoubted faith, called the "Clerk," to communicate with students of universities, and a youth called a "Friend," to influence the people; but neither the Clerk nor the Friend were initiated into the mysteries of the order. Every council assumed a particular name, such as "Virtue," "Honour," "Loyalty," and met, as if for amusement only, without apparatus or writing of any kind. A supreme council sat at Bologna; there were councils at Florence, Venice, Milan, Naples, etc. They endeavoured to gain adherents, who should be ignorant of the existence of the society, and should yet further its ends. Lucien Bonaparte is said to have been a "great light" among them. Their object was the independence of Italy, to be effected by means of all the secret societies of the country united under the leadership of the Guelphs.

376. *Guelphs and Carbonari.*—The Guelphs found powerful helpers in the Carbonari; we might indeed call the former a high vendita or lodge of the latter.

And the chiefs of the Carbonari were also chiefs among the Guelphs; but only those that had distinct offices among the Carbonari could be admitted among the Guelphs. There can be no doubt that the Carbonari, when the sect had become very numerous, partly sheltered themselves under the designation of Guelphs and Adelphi or Independents, by affiliating themselves to these societies.

377. *The Independents.*—Though these also aimed at the independence of Italy, yet it appears that they were not disinclined to effect it by means of foreign assistance. The report at that time was that they actually once intended to offer the crown of Italy to the Duke of Wellington; but this is highly improbable, since our Iron Duke was not at all popular in Italy. But it is highly probable that they sought the co-operation of Russia, which, since 1815, maintained many agents in Italy—with what purpose is not exactly known; the collection of statistical and economical information was the ostensible object, but Austria looked on them with a very suspicious eye, and watched them narrowly. The Independents had close relations with these Russian agents, probably, as it is surmised, with a view of turning Russian influence to account in any outbreak against Austria.

378. *The Delphic Priesthood.*—This was another secret society, having the same political object as the foregoing. The Delphic priest, the patriotic

priest, the priest militant, spoke thus:—" My mother has the sea for her mantle, high mountains for her sceptre ;" and when asked who his mother was, replied :—" The lady with the dark tresses, whose gifts are beauty, wisdom, and formerly strength; whose dowry is a flourishing garden, full of fragrant flowers, where bloom the olive and the vine; and who now groans, stabbed to the heart." The Delphics entertained singular hopes, and would invoke the "remedy of the ocean" (American auxiliaries), and the epoch of "cure" (a general European war). They called the partisans of France "pagans," and those of Austria, "monsters ;" the Germans they styled "savages." Their place of meeting they designated as the "ship," to foreshadow the future maritime greatness of Italy, and the help they expected from over the sea; their chief was the "pilot."

379. *The Latini.*—This sect existed about 1817. Only those initiated into the higher degrees of Carbonarism could become members. In their oath they declared :—" I swear to employ every means in my power to further the happiness of Italy. I swear religiously to keep the secret and fulfil the duties of this society, and never to do aught that could compromise its safety ; and that I will only act in obedience to its decisions. If ever I violate this oath, I will submit to whatever punishment the society may inflict, even to death."

II.

NAPOLEONISM AND ANTI-NAPOLEONISM.

380.

THE Rays.—During the power of Napoleon, he was opposed by secret societies in Italy, as well as in France. But his fall, which to many seemed a revival of liberty, to others appeared as the ruin of Italy; hence they sought to re-establish his rule, or at least to save Italian nationality from the wreck. The " Rays" were an Anti-Napoleonic society, composed of officials from all parts, brought together by common dangers and the adventures of the field. They had lodges at Milan and Bologna.

381. *Societies in Favour of Napoleon.*—Many societies in favour of the restoration of Napoleon were formed, such as the " Black Needle," the " Knights of the Sun," " Universal Regeneration," etc. They were generally composed of the soldiers of the great captain, who were condemned to inacti-

vity, and looked upon the glory of their chief as something in which they had a personal interest. Their aim was to place Napoleon at the head of confederated Italy, under the title of " Emperor of Rome, by the will of the people and the grace of God." The proposal reached him early in the year 1815. Napoleon accepted it like a man who on being shipwrecked perceives a piece of wood that may save him, and which he will cast into the fire when he has reached the land. The effects of these plots are known—Napoleon's escape from Elba, and the reign of a hundred days.

382. *The Centres.*—An offshoot of Carbonarism was the society formed in Lombardy, under the designation of the " Centres." Nothing was to be written; and conversation on the affairs of the order was only to take place between two members at a time, who recognised each other by the words, " Succour to the unfortunate," and by raising the hand three times to the forehead, in sign of grief. The Centres once more revived the hopes of Murat. A rising was to take place under his auspices against the detested Austrians; the ringing of the bells of Milan was to be the signal for the outbreak; and it is said that "Vespers" had been arranged, from which no Austrian was to escape alive. But on the appointed day fear or horror held the hand that was to have given the signal, that of General Fontanelli. Hence, fatal delay and the discovery of the secret.

For Bellegarde or Talleyrand sent a certain Viscount Saint-Aignan among the conspirators, who after having discovered all their plans, betrayed them to Austria, and was never heard of again. Austria seized the ringleaders and instituted proceedings against them, which lasted about three years, and were finally closed by delivering—it is not known why—very mild sentences against the conspirators.

III.

SOUTHERN PROVINCES.

383.

VARIOUS Societies.—Sicily did not escape the general influence. In 1827 there was formed a secret society in favour of the Greek revolution, the "Friends of Greece," who, however, also occupied themselves with the affairs of Italy. There was also the "Secret Society of the Five," founded ten years before the above, which prepared the insurrection of the Greeks. In Messina was formed the lodge of the "Patriotic Reformers," founded on Carbonarism, which corresponded with lodges at Florence, Milan, and Turin, by means of musical notes.

384. *Italian Littérateurs.*—This sect, introduced into Palermo in 1823, had neither signs nor distinctive marks. In every town there was a delegate, called the "Radical," who could affiliate unto himself ten others or more, acquiring the name of "decurion," or " centurion." The initiated were

called " sons," who in their turn could affiliate unto themselves ten others, and these could do the same in their turn ; so that thus a mighty association was formed. The initiated were called " Brethren Barabbas," Christ representing the tyrant, and Barabbas the people—a singular confusion of ideas, by which the victim slain on the cross for the redemption of human conscience and thought was considered as an example and upholder of tyranny. But it was a symbolism which concealed juster ideas and more conformable with truth. They recognised each other by means of a ring, and attested their letters by the well-known initials I. N. R. I. The Society was much feared and jealously watched, and helped to fill the prisons. It only ceased when other circumstances called forth other societies.

385. *Societies in Calabria and the Abruzzi.*—These districts, by their natural features and the disposition of their inhabitants, were at all times the favourite resorts of conspirators. We there find the sects of the " European Patriots or White Pilgrims," the " Philadelphians," and the " Decisi," who thence spread into other Italian provinces, with military organization, arms, and commanders. The first two partly came from France; nor were their operations, as the names intimate, confined to the peninsula. The lodges of the " Decisi" (Decided) were called " Decisions," as the assemblies of the Patriots were called " Squadrons," each from forty to sixty

strong, and those of the Philadelphians, "Camps." The Decisi, whose numbers amounted perhaps to forty thousand, held their meetings at night, carefully guarded by sentinels; and their military exercises took place in solitary houses, or suppressed convents. Their object was to fall upon Naples and proclaim a republic; but circumstances were not propitious. Their leader, Ciro Annichiarico, a priest, was a man of great resources and vast influence, so that it was necessary to despatch against him General Church, who captured him and had him shot. As Ciro was rather a remarkable personage, a brief account of him may not be uninteresting.

386. *Ciro Annichiarico.*—This priest was driven from society by his crimes. He was accused of murder, committed in a fit of jealousy, and sentenced to fifteen years of exile, although there is strong reason to believe that he was innocent and was made the victim of party-spirit. Instead of being permitted, according to the sentence, to leave the country, he was for four years kept in prison, whence at last he made his escape—took refuge in the mountain forests, and placed himself at the head of a band of outlaws, and, as his enemies declare, committed all kinds of enormities. At Martano, they say, he penetrated into one of the first houses of the place, and, after having offered violence to its mistress, massacred her with all her people,

and carried off 96,000 ducats. He was in correspondence with all the brigands; and whoever wished to get rid of an enemy, had only to address himself to Ciro. On being asked, after his capture, how many persons he had killed with his own hand, he carelessly answered :—" Who can remember ? Perhaps sixty or seventy." His activity, artifice, and intrepidity were astonishing. He was a first-rate shot and rider; his singular good fortune in extricating himself from the most imminent dangers acquired for him the reputation of a necromancer upon whom ordinary means of attack had no power. Though a priest himself, and exercising the functions of one when he thought it expedient, he was rather a libertine, and declared his clerical colleagues to be impostors without any faith. He published a paper against the missionaries, who, according to him, disseminated illiberal opinions among the people, and forbade them on pain of death to preach in the villages, " because, instead of the true principles of the Gospel they taught nothing but fables and impostures." Probably Ciro was pretty correct in his estimate of their performances. He could be generous on occasions. One day he surprised General d'Octavio, a Corsican, in the service of Murat—who pursued him for a long time with a thousand men—walking alone in a garden. Ciro discovered himself, remarking, that the life of the general, who was unarmed, was in his hands; " but," said he, " I will pardon you this time, although I shall no longer be so indulgent if you continue to hunt me about." So saying, he leaped over the wall and disappeared. His physiognomy was rather agreeable; he was of middle stature, well made and very strong. He had a verbose eloquence. Extremely addicted to pleasure, he had mistresses, at the period of his power, in all the towns of the province over which he was continually ranging. When King Ferdinand returned to his states on this side the Taro, he recalled such as had been exiled for political opinions. Ciro attempted to pass for one of these, but a new order of arrest was issued against him. It was then that he placed himself at the head of the Decisi. Many excesses are laid to their charge. A horde of twenty or thirty of them over-ran the country in disguise, masked as punchinellos. In places where open force could not be employed, the most daring were sent to watch for the moment to execute the sentences of secret death pronounced by the society. It was thus that the justice of the peace of Luogo Rotondo and his wife were killed in their own garden; and that the sectary, Perone, plunged his knife into the bowels of an old man of seventy, and afterwards massacred his wife and servant, having introduced himself into their house under pretence of delivering a letter. As has already been intimated, it was finally found necessary to send an armed force, under the command of

General Church, against this band of ruffians. Many of them having been taken, and the rest dispersed, Ciro, with only three companions, took refuge in one of the fortified farm-houses near Francavilla, but after a vigorous defence was obliged to surrender. The Council of War, by which he was tried, condemned him to be shot. A missionary offered him the consolations of religion. Ciro answered him with a smile :—" Let us leave alone this prating ; we are of the same profession ; don't let us laugh at one another." On his arrival at the place of execution, Ciro wished to remain standing ; he was told to kneel, and did so, presenting his breast. He was then informed that malefactors like himself were shot with their backs to the soldiers ; he submitted, at the same time advising a priest, who persisted in remaining near him, to withdraw, so as not to expose himself. Twenty-one balls took effect, four in the head, yet he still breathed and muttered in his throat ; the twenty-second put an end to him. This fact was confirmed by all the officers and soldiers present at his death. "As soon as we perceived," said a soldier very gravely, " that he was enchanted, we loaded his own musket with a silver ball, and this destroyed the spell." After the death of the leader, some two hundred and thirty persons were brought to trial ; nearly half of them,, having been guilty of murder and robbery with violence, were condemned to capital punishment, and their heads exposed near the places of their residence, or in the scene of their crimes.

387. *Certificates of the Decisi.*—To render the account of the Decisi as complete as it need be, I subjoin a copy of one of their Patents or Certificates :—

Tristezza.   Morte.

Death's Head.   S(alentina).   D(ecisione).   (Seal.)   Death's Head.
(*S*alute).

N° V. Grandi Muratori.

L. D. D. G. T.—E. D. T. D. U.[1]

Il Mortale Gaetano Caffieri è un *F. D. N*umero Quinto, appartenente alla *D* dcl *T*onante *G*iove, sparsa sulla superficie della *T*erra, per la sua *D* avuto il piacere di far parte in questa *R. S. D. N*oi dunque invitiamo tutte le *S*ocietà *F*ilantropiche a prestar il loro braccio forte al medesimo ed a soccorlo ne' suoi bisogni, essendo egli giunto alla *D* di acquistare la *L*ibertà o *M*orte. *O*ggi li 29 *O*ttobre 1817.

Pietro Gargaro.   *Il G. M. D. N°.* 1.

. . . .

V°. de Serio 2° Deciso

Gaetano Caffieri
Cross bones.   Registratore de' Morti.   (Seal.)   Cross bones.
Terror.   Struggle.

That is : La Decisione di Giove Tonante—Esterminatore dei Tiranni dell' Universo.

Translation.

The Salentine Decision.

Health!

No. 5, Grand Masons.

The Decision of Jupiter Tonaus (the name of the lodge) hopes to make war against the tyrants of the universe, &c.

The mortal Gaetano Caffieri is a Brother Decided, No. 5, belonging to the Decision of Jupiter the Thunderer, spread over the face of the earth, has had the pleasure to belong to this Salentine Republican Decision. We invite, there-fore, all Philanthropic Societies to lend their strong arm to the same, and to assist him in his wants, he having come to the decision to obtain · liberty or death. Dated this day, the 29th October, 1817.

Pietro Gargaro, the Decided Grand Master, No. 1.

Vito de Serio, Second Decided.

Gaetano Caffieri, Registrar of the Dead.

The letters in italics in the original were written in blood. The upper seal represents fasces planted upon a death's head, surmounted by the Phrygian cap and flanked by hatchets; the lower, thunderbolts casting down royal and imperial crowns and the tiara. The person in whose favour the certificate is issued, figures himself among the signatures with the title of Registrar of the Dead, that is of those they immolated to their vengeance, of whom they kept a register apart. The four points observable after the signature of Pietro Gargaro indicate his power of passing sentence of death. When the Decisi wrote to any one to extort contributions, if they added these four points, it was known that the person they addressed was condemned to death in case of disobedience. If the points were not added he was threatened with milder punishment. Their colours, yellow, red, and blue, surrounded the patent.

388. *Various other Societies*—The society of the " Shirtless," founded by a Frenchman of the name of Manuel, who invoked Samson, as the symbol of strength, had but a very short existence. That of the " Spectres meeting in a Tomb," which existed in 1822, and whose object was the overthrow of the Bourbons, also came to a speedy end. The " New Reform of France," and the " Provinces," which were probably founded in 1820, only admitted members already initiated into Carbonarism, Freemasonry, the European Patriots, or the Greeks in Solitude. A mixture of many sects, they condensed the hatred of many ages and many orders against tyranny, and prescribed the following oath :—" I. M. N., promise and swear to be the eternal enemy of tyrants, to entertain undying hatred against them, and, when opportunity offers, to slay them." In their succinct catechism were the following passages :—
" Who art thou ?" " Thy friend." " How knowest thou me ?" " By the weight pressing on thy brow, on which I read written in letters of blood, To conquer or die." " What wilt thou ?" " Destroy the thrones and raise up gibbets." " By what right ?" " By that of nature." " For what purpose ?" " To

acquire the glorious name of citizen." "And wilt thou risk thy life?" "I value life less than liberty."

Another sect was that of the "New French Liberals," which existed but a short time. It was composed of but few members, but they were men of some standing, chiefly such as had occupied high positions under Napoleon. They also looked to America for assistance. They wore a small black ribbon attached to their watches, with a gold seal, a piece of coral, and an iron or steel ring. The ribbon symbolized the eternal hatred of the free for oppressors; the coral, their American hopes; the ring, the weapon to destroy their enemies; and the gold seal, abundance of money as a means of success.

IV.

THE CLERICS.

389.

THE Consistorials.—But the conspirators against thrones and the Church were not to have it all their own way; clerical associations were formed to counteract their efforts. The sect of the "Consistorials" aimed at the preservation of feudal and theocratic dominion. The rich and ambitious patricians of Rome and other Italian states belonged to it; Tabot, an ex-Jesuit and Confessor to the Holy Father, was the ruling spirit. It is said that this society proposed to give to the Pope, Tuscany; the island of Elba and the Marches, to the King of Naples; Parma, Piacenza, and a portion of Lombardy, with the title of King, to the Duke of Modena; the rest of Lombardy, Massa Carrara, and Lucca, to the King of Sardinia; and to Russia, which, from jealousy of Austria, favoured these secret designs, either Ancona, or Genoa, or Civita Vecchia, to turn it into their Gibraltar. From documents found in the office of the Austrian governor at Milan, it appears that the Duke of Modena, in 1818, presided at a general meeting of the Consistorials, and that Austria was aware of the existence and intentions of the society.

390. *The Roman Catholic Apostolic Congregation.*—It was formed at the period of the imprisonment of Pius VII. The members recognized each other by a yellow silk ribbon with five knots; the initiated into the lower degrees heard of nothing but acts of piety and charity; the secrets of the society, known to the higher ranks, could only be discussed between two; the lodges were composed of five members, the pass-word was "Eleutheria," *i. e.* Liberty; and the secret word "Ode," *i. e.* Independence. This sect arose in France, among the Neocatholics, led by Lammenais, who already, in the treatise on "Religious Indifference," had shown that fervour which afterwards was to carry him so far. Thence it passed into Lombardy, but met with but little success, and the Austrians succeeded in obtaining the patents which were given to the initiated, and their statutes and signs of recognition. Though devoted to the independence of Italy, the Congregation was not factious; for it bound the destinies of nations to the full triumph of the Roman Catholic religion. Narrow in scope, and restricted

in numbers, it neither possessed, nor perhaps claimed, powers to subvert the political system.

391. *Sanfedisti.*—This society was founded at the epoch of the suppression of the Jesuits. There existed long before then in the Papal States a society called the "Pacific" or "Holy Union," which was established to defend religion, the privileges and jurisdiction of Rome, and the temporal power of the popes. Now from this society they derived the appellation of the Society of the Holy Faith, or *Sanfedisti.* They conspired against Napoleon, who sent about twenty of them to prison at Modena, whence they were released by Francis IV. The supposed chiefs, after 1815, were the Duke of Modena and Cardinal Consalvi. The first had frequent secret interviews with the cardinals, and even the King of Sardinia was said to be in the plot. Large sums also are said to have been contributed by the chiefs to carry on the war against Austria, which however is doubtful. Some attribute to this society the project of dividing Italy into three kingdoms, expelling the Austrians and the King of Naples; others, the intention of dividing it into five, viz., Sardinia, Modena, Lucca, Rome, and Naples; and yet others—and these latter probably are most in the right—the determination to perpetuate the *status quo*, or to re-establish servitude in its most odious forms. They also intrigued with Russia, though at certain times they would not have objected

to subject all Italy politically to the Austrian eagle, and clerically to the keys of St. Peter. Their machinations at home led to much internal dissension and bloodshed; their chief opponents were the Carbonari. At Faenza the two parties fought against one another under the names of " Cats" and " Dogs." They caused quite as much mischief and bloodshed as any of the bands of brigands that infested the country, and their code was quite as sanguinary as that of any more secular society. They swore with terrible oaths to pursue and slay the impious liberals, even to their children, without showing pity for age or sex. Under the pretence of defending the faith, they indulged in the grossest licentiousness and most revolting atrocity. In the Papal States they were under the direction of the inquisitors and bishops; in the kingdom of Naples under the immediate orders of the police.

392. *The Calderari.*—This Society, alluded to before (360), is of uncertain origin. Count Orloff, in his work, " Memoirs on the Kingdom of Naples," says they arose in 1813, when the reform of Carbonarism took place. Canosa, on the other hand, in a pamphlet published at Dublin, and entitled, " The Mountain Pipes," says they arose at Palermo, and not at Naples. In the former of these towns, there existed different trade companies, which had enjoyed great privileges, until they lost them by the constitution of Lord William Bentinck. The

numerous company of braziers (*calderari*) felt the loss most keenly ; and they sent a deputation to the Queen of Naples, assuring her that they were ready to rise in her defence. The flames of the insurrection were communicated to the tanners and other companies, and all the Neapolitan emigrants in Sicily. Lord William Bentinck put the emigrants on board ship and sent them under a neutral flag to Naples, where Murat received them very kindly. But they were not grateful. Immediately on their arrival they entered into the secret societies then conspiring against the French government, and their original name of Calderari was communicated by them to the conspirators, before then called " Trinitarii." We have seen that on the return of Ferdinand, Prince Canova favoured the Calderari. He styled them the Calderari of the Counterpoise, because they were to serve as such to Carbonarism. The fate of Canova and that of the Calderari has already been mentioned (360, 361).

393. *Societies in Favour of Napoleonism.*—In the unsettled state of political affairs, every party found its adherents. According to secret documents lately discovered, the machinations of the Bonapartists continued even in 1842, the leaders being Peter Bouaparte, Lady Christina Stuart, the daughter of Lucien Bonaparte, the Marchioness Pepoli, the daughter of the Countess Lipona (Caroline Murat), and Count Rasponi. Then

appeared the sect of the "Italian Confederates," which in 1842 extended into Spain. Another sect, the "Illuminati, Vindicators or Avengers of the People," arose in the Papal States; also those of "Regeneration," of "Italian Independence," of the "Communists," the "Exterminators," &c. Tuscany also had its secret societies—that of the "Thirty-one," the "National Knights," the "Revolutionary Club," &c. A "Communistic Society" was formed at Milan; but none of these sects did more than excite a little curiosity for a time. Scarcely anything of their ritual is known.

394. *Apostolate of Dante.*—One of the most recent societies of the Romagna was that of the "Apostolate of Dante," which sought, in the name of that poet, to spread national ideas. The leading spirit was Tamburini, a well-known patriot; and many men of note in politics and letters joined the society, which was founded in 1855. But in December, 1856, Tamburini and all his companions were arrested. The legal proceedings against them lasted thirty-three months, and ended by the condemnation of Tamburini and another to twenty years' incarceration, and to ten years' of the others. Pius IX., though entreated by the judges themselves, refused to mitigate the punishment. But in 1859 the five youngest were set free, and Tamburini was released by the people in 1860.

V.

CENTRAL ITALY AND LOMBARDY.

395.

AMERICAN Hunters.—The Society of the "American Hunters" was founded at Ravenna, shortly after the prosecutions of Macerata (362), and the measures taken by the Austrian government, in 1818, against the Carbonari. Lord Byron is said to have been at its head, having imbibed his love for Italy through the influence of an Italian beauty, the Countess Guiccioli, whose brother had been exiled a few years before. Its ceremonies assimilated it to the "Comuneros" of Spain (422), and it seems to have had the same aims as the Delphic Priesthood (378). The saviour was to come from America, and it is asserted that Joseph Bonaparte, the ex-King of Spain, was a member of the society. It is not improbable that the partizans of Napoleon gathered new hopes after the events of 1815. A sonnet, of which the first quatrain is here given, was at that time very popular in Central Italy, and shows the direction of the political wind :—

" Scandalized by groaning under kings so fell,
    Filling Europe with dismay in ev'ry part,
    We are driven to solicit Bonaparte
To return from Saint Helena or from hell."

The restored sect made itself the centre of many minor sects, among which were the " Sons of Mars," so called because composed chiefly of military men ; of the " Artist Brethren ; " " the Defenders of the Country ; " the " Friends of Duty ; " and others, having the simpler and less compromising forms of Carbonarism. In the sect of the " Sons of Mars," the old Carbonari vendita was called " bivouac ; " the apprentice, " volunteer ;" the good cousin, " corporal ;" the master, " sergeant ;" the grand master, " commander ;" and the chief dignitaries of Carbonarism still governed, from above and unseen, the thoughts of the sect. Many other sects existed of which scarcely more than the names are known, the recapitulation of which would only weary the reader.

396. *Secret Italian Society in London.*—London was a great centre of the sectaries. In 1822, a society for liberating Italy from the Austrian yoke was formed in that city, counting among its members many distinguished Italian patriots. Austria took the alarm, and sent spies to discover their plans. These spies represented the operations of the society

as very extensive and imminent. An expedition was to sail from the English coasts for Spain, to take on board a large number of adherents, land them on the Italian shores and spread insurrection everywhere. The English general, Robert Wilson, was said to be at the head of the expedition; of which, however, nothing was ever heard, and the Austrian government escaped with the mere fright.

397. *Secret Italian Societies in Paris.*—A society of Italians was formed in Paris, in 1829; and in 1830, French Liberals formed a society under the title of " Cosmopolitans," whose object was to revolutionize all the peoples of the Latin race, and form them into one grand confederacy. La Fayette was at its head. But where are the results ?

VI.

THE EXILES.

398.

GYPTIAN Lodges.—Immediately after the downfall of Napoleon, societies were formed also in foreign countries to promote Italian independence. The promoters of these were chiefly exiles. Distant Egypt even became the centre of such a propaganda; and under the auspices of Mehemet Ali, who aspired to render himself independent of the Sublime Porte, there was established the Egyptian rite of Cagliostro with many variations, and under the title of the "Secret Egyptian Society." Under masonic forms, the Pacha hoped to further his own views; and especially, to produce political changes in the Ionian Islands and in Italy, he scattered his agents all over the Mediterranean coasts. Being masonic, the society excluded no religion; it retained the two annual festivals, and added a third in memory of Napoleon, whose portrait was honoured in the lodge.

The rites were chiefly those of the ancient and accepted Scotch. Women were admitted, Turks excluded; and in the lodges of Alexandria and Cairo, the Greek and Arab women amounted to more than three hundred. The emissaries, spread over many parts of Europe, corresponded in cypher; but of the operations of the society nothing was ever positively known.

399. *The Illuminati.*—This society, not to be confounded with an earlier one of the same name (316 *et seq.*), was founded in France, but meeting with too many obstacles in that country, it spread all over Italy. Its object was to restore the Napoleon family to the French throne, by making Marie-Louise regent, until the King of Rome could be set on the throne, and by bringing Napoleon himself from St. Helena, to command the army: The society entered into correspondence with Las Casas, who was to come to Bologna, the chief lodge, and arrange plans; but the scheme, as need scarcely be mentioned, never came to anything.

BOOK XVI.

YOUTH.

There were days, when my heart was volcanic,
  As the scoriac rivers that roll,
  As the lavas, that restlessly roll
Their sulphurous currents down Yanik,
  In the clime of the boreal pole;
That groan as they roll down mount Yanik,
  In the clime of the ultimate pole.

E. A. Poe.

AUTHORITIES.

Contemporary journalism of various countries.

Mazzini. Scritti editi e inediti. Milan, 1861-3.

Histoire de l'Internationale. Par Jacques Populus. Paris, 1871.

La Fin du Bonapartisme. Par E. de Pompery. Paris, 1872.

La Comune di Parigi nel 1871. Per J. Cantù. Milano, 1873.

Histoire de l'Internationale. Par E. Villetard. Paris, 1872.

Secret History of the International. By Onslow Yorke. London, 1872.

I.

YOUNG POLAND.

400.

POLISH *Patriotism.*—It is the fashion to express great sympathy with the Poles and a corresponding degree of indignation against Russia; the Poles are looked upon as a patriotic race, oppressed by their more powerful neighbour. But all this rests on mere misapprehension and ignorance of facts. The Polish people under their native rulers were abject serfs. The aristocracy were everything, and possessed everything; the people possessed nothing, not even political or civil rights, when these clashed with the whims or interests of the nobles. It is these last whose power has been overthrown—it is they who make war on and conspire against Russia, to recover their ancient privileges over their own countrymen, who blindly, like most nations, allow themselves to be slaughtered for the benefit of those who only seek again to rivet on the limbs of their dupes the chains

which Russia has broken.   It is like the French
and Spaniards and Neapolitans fighting against their
deliverer Napoleon, to bring back the Bourbon
tyrants, and with them the people's political nullity,
clerical intolerance, *lettres de çachet,* and the Inquisition.   How John Bull has been gulled by these
Polish patriots!   Many of them were criminals of
all kinds, who succeeded in breaking out of prison,
or escaping before they could be captured; and,
managing to come over to this country, have here
called themselves political fugitives, victims of Russian persecution, and have lived luxuriously on the
credulity of Englishmen!

401. *Various Revolutionary Sects.*—One of the
first societies formed in Poland to organize the
revolutionary forces of the country was that of the
" True Poles ; " but, consisting of few persons only,
it did not last long.   In 1818 another sect arose,
that of " National Freemasonry," which borrowed
the rites, degrees, and language of Freemasonry, but
aimed at national independence.   The society was
open to persons of all classes, but sought chiefly to
enlist soldiers and officials, so as to turn their
technical knowledge to account in the day of the
struggle.   But though numerous, the society lasted
only a few years; for disunion arose among the
members, and it escaped total dissolution only by
transformation.   It altered its rites and ceremonies,
and henceforth called itself the " Scythers," in

remembrance of the revolution of 1794, in which whole regiments, armed with scythes, had gone into battle. They met in 1821 at Warsaw, and drew up a new revolutionary scheme, adopting at the same time the new denomination of "Patriotic Society." In the meanwhile the students of the university of Wilna had formed themselves into a secret society; which, however, was discovered by the Russian government and dissolved. In 1822 the Patriotic Society combined with the masonic rite of "Modern Templars," founded in Poland by Captain Maiewski; to the three rites of symbolical masonry was added a fourth, in which the initiated swore to do all in his power towards the liberation of his country. These combined societies brought about the insurrection of 1830. In 1834 was established the society of "Young Poland;" one of its most distinguished members and chiefs being Simon Konarski, who had already distinguished himself in the insurrection of 1830. He then made his escape, and in order better to conceal himself learnt the art of watchmaking. Having returned to Poland and joined "Young Poland," he was discovered in 1838, and subjected to the torture to extort from him the names of his accomplices. But no revelations could be obtained from him, and he bore his sufferings with such courage that the military governor of Wilna exclaimed:—"This is a man of iron!" A Russian officer offered to assist him in escaping, and being detected, was sent to the Caucasian army for life. Konarski was executed in 1839, the people tearing his clothes to pieces to possess a relic of him. The chains he had been loaded with were formed into rings and worn by his admirers. Men like these redeem the sins of many so-called " Polish patriots."

402. *Secret national government.* — Some time before the outbreak of the Crimean war a secret national government was formed in Poland, of course with the object of organizing an insurrection against Russia. Little was known for a long time about their proceedings. Strange stories were circulated of midnight meetings in subterranean passages ; of traitors condemned by courts composed of masked and hooded judges, from whose sentence there was no appeal and no escape ; of domiciliary visits from which neither the palace nor the hovel was exempt ; and of corpses found nightly in the most crowded streets of the city, or on the loneliest wastes of the open country, the dagger which had killed the victim bearing a label stamped with the well-known device of the insurrectionary committee. So perfectly was the secret of the modern Vehmgericht kept that the Russian police were completely baffled in their attempts to discover its members. At that period the Poles were divided into two parties :—the " whites " and the " reds ;" the former representing the aristocratic, the latter the democratic element of the nation. Each had its own

organization. The whites were mostly in favour
of strictly constitutional resistance; the reds were
for open rebellion and an immediate appeal to arms.
But a union was brought about between the two
parties in consequence of the conscription introduced by Russia into Poland in 1863, which set fire
to the train of rebellion that had so long been
preparing. But Langiewicz, the Polish leader,
having been defeated, the movements of the insurgents in the open field were arrested; though the
rebellion was prolonged in other ways, chiefly with a
view of inducing the Western Powers to interfere in
behalf of Poland. But these naturally thought that
as the Polish people, the peasantry, had taken very
little share in the insurrection, and as Alexander II.
had really introduced a series of reforms which
materially improved the position of his Polish subjects, there was no justification for the outbreak;
and therefore allowed justice to take its course.

II.

THE UNION OF SAFETY.

403.

*H*ISTORICAL *Sketch of Society.*——Russia has ever been a hot-bed of secret societies, but to within very recent times such societies were purely local; the Russian people might revolt against some local oppression, or some subaltern tyrant, but they never rose against the emperor, they never took up arms for a political question. Whatever secret associations were formed in that country, moreover, were formed by the aristocracy, and many of them were of the most innocent nature; it was at one time almost fashionable to belong to such a society, as there are people now who fancy it an honour to be a Freemason. But after the wars of Napoleon, the sectarian spirit spread into Russia. Some of the officers of the

Russian army, after their campaigns in Central Europe, on their return to their native country, felt their own degradation and the oppression under which they existed; and conceived the desire to free themselves from the same. In 1822 the then government of Russia issued a decree, prohibiting the formation of a new, or the continuance of old secret societies. The decree embraced the masonic lodges. Every employé of the state was obliged to declare on oath that he belonged to no secret society within or without the empire; or, if he did, had immediately to break off all connection with them, on pain of dismissal. The decree was executed with great rigour; the furniture of the masonic lodges was sold in the open streets, so as to expose the mysteries of masonry to ridicule. When the state began to prohibit secret societies, it was time to form some in right earnest. Alexander Mouravief founded the *Union of Safety*, whose rites and ceremonies were chiefly masonic, frightful oaths, daggers and poison figuring largely therein. It was composed of three classes—Brethren, Men, and Boyards. The chiefs were taken from the last class. The denomination of the last degree shows how much the aristocratic element predominated in the association, which led in fact to the formation of a society still more aristocratic, that of the " Russian Knights," which aimed at obtaining for the Russian people a constitutional charter, and counteracting the secret societies of Poland, whose object was to restore Poland to its ancient state, that is to say, absolutism on the part of the nobles, and abject slavery on the part of the people. The two societies eventually coalesced into one under the denomination of the "Union of the Public Good;" but, divided in its counsels, it was dissolved in 1821, and a new society formed under the title of the "Union of the Boyards." The programme of this union at first was to reduce the imperial power to a level with that of the president of the United States, and to form the empire into a federation of provinces. But gradually their views became more advanced; a republic was proposed, and the emperor was to be put to death. The more moderate and respectable members withdrew from the society, and after a short time it was dissolved, and its papers and documents carefully burnt. The revolutions of Spain, Naples, and Upper Italy led Pestal, a man who had been a member of all the former secret societies, to form a new one, with the view of turning Russia into a republic; the death of Alexander again formed part of the scheme. But circumstances were not favourable to the conspirators, and the project fell to the ground. Another society, called the *North*, sprang into existence, of which Pestal again was the leading spirit. In 1824, the " Union of Boyards " heard of the existence of the Polish Patriotic Society.   It was determined to invite their co-operation.   The terms were speedily arranged. The Boyards bound themselves to acknowledge the independence of Poland; and the Poles promised to entertain or amuse the arch-duke Constantine at Warsaw whilst the revolution was being accomplished in Russia.   Both countries were to adopt the republican form of government. This latter condition, however, made by the Poles, displeased the Boyards, who, themselves lusting after power, did not see in a republic the opportunity of achieving it.   The Boyards therefore united themselves with another society, that of the ` " United Slavonians," founded in 1823, by a lieutenant of artillery, named Borissoff, small in numbers, but daring. As the name implied, it proposed a Slavonian confederation.   The insurrection was on the point of breaking out; but was denounced by Captain Mayboroda. The Russian government had its first victim, Pestal, and the scheme was put off until a more favourable opportunity. The death of Alexander found the conspirators unprepared. Reorganized, they formed new plots; and on the 14th of December, 1825, several regiments issued from their barracks to attack the legitimate power.   But they were beaten and decimated; five of the conspirators were executed, and thousands sent to Siberia.   Still secret societies continued to exist. One was discovered at Moscow. in 1838, a remnant of that which was broken up in 1825. Its members consisted of some of the highest nobles of the empire, who were scattered in the army as private soldiers.

404. *Nihilists.*—This secret revolutionary society, lately discovered in Russia, and many members of which were seized and condemned to various punishments, very slight in comparison with the offences charged against them, had for its object the overthrow of the constitution, and the establishment of universal Communism. The following articles, taken from a document produced at the trial, and containing the programme of what these Socialist reformers intended, will show that they belonged to the most advanced school of revolutionism :—

" 1. The Revolutionist is a man condemned. He can have no interests, nor business, nor feelings, nor attachments, nor property, nor even a name. Everything in him is absorbed in one sole and exclusive interest, in one single idea, in one solitary passion—the Revolution.

" 2. In his own mind he has broken, not alone in words but in fact, every bond with civil order and with the whole civilized world, with all laws, all customs and conventions, and all the moral rules of the world. He is towards that world a pitiless enemy, and if he continues to live in it it is only that he may the more certainly destroy it.

" 3. The Revolutionist despises all doctrines, and has renounced all science of this world, which he leaves to future generations. He knows but one science, that of destruction."

" 5. The Revolutionist is a condemned man, devoid of pity towards the state and the enlightened classes of society, neither does he expect any mercy from them. Between them and himself there is waged a death struggle, open or concealed, but continuous and implacable. He must learn to suffer tortures.

" 6. Severe towards himself, he must be severe towards others. All tender and effeminate feelings of family, friendship, love, gratitude, and even of honour, must often be stifled in his breast by the one cold passion of Revolution. For him there is but one repose, but one consolation, but one recompense, but one satisfaction, the success of the Revolution. By day and by night he must have but one thought, but one single object—destruction without mercy."

" 8. The Revolutionist can have no friend, and cannot regard any but men who have applied themselves to the Revolutionary work like himself. The degree of friendship, of devotion, and of other obligations towards a like companion is determined solely by the degree of usefulness for the work of practical Revolution, destructive of everything."

" 10. Each companion should have at his disposal a number of Revolutionists of the second or third class—that is to say, not completely initiated. He must look upon them as part of the Revolutionary capital placed at his disposal.

" 11. When a companion falls into misfortune, and it becomes a question whether or not he shall be saved, the Revolutionist must consult not his personal feelings, but only the interest of the Revolutionary cause. He must, therefore, balance the amount of usefulness represented by such companion against the loss of the Revolutionary force necessary to save him, and should decide according to weight and value."

The society embraced men of every rank of life, the leading spirit being Netchaiev, who escaped. Dolgow, the next in·importance, was the son of a counsellor, and these two succeeded in tainting with their opinions the views of many of the students at the Petrovsky University. They were seconded in their efforts by Rippona, the son of a military officer, and Prince Cherkésoff, who on several occasions supplied the funds required. Their plans were secretly made known to the friends of the movement by means of a paper entitled, " From the United to the Isolated," which called on the Russians to revolt against the government. In spite of this, the sentences on the prisoners, who were all found guilty, as above stated, were exceedingly mild, the severest being that on Prince Cherkésoff, who was deprived of his rights and privileges, and ordered to take up his abode in the province of Towsk for the space of five years. The other conspirators were condemned to periods of imprisonment, varying from a year and a half to three weeks.

III.

THE UNION OF VIRTUE.

405.

GERMAN *Feeling against Napoleon.*— Napoleon, whilst he could in Germany form a court composed of kings and princes obedient to his slightest nod, also found implacable and incorruptible individualities, who swore undying hatred to him who ruled half the world. Still, those who opposed the French emperor had no determined plan, and were misled by fallacious hopes; and the leaders, always clever in taking advantage of the popular forces, threw the more daring ones in front like a vanguard, whose destruction is pre-determined, in order to fill up the chasm that separates the main body from victory.

406. *Formation and Scope of Tugendbund.*—Two of the men who were the first, or amongst the first, to meditate the downfal of the conqueror before whom all German governments had fallen prostrate, were Count Stadion, the soul of Austrian politics,

and Baron Stein, a native of Nassau, who possessed great influence at the Prussian Court. The latter, devoted to monarchical institutions, but also to the independence of his country, groaned when he saw the Prussian government degraded in the eyes of Europe, and undertook to avenge its humiliation by founding, in 1812, the secret society of the " Union of Virtue " (*Tugendbund*), whose first domiciles were at Königsberg and Breslau. Napoleon's police discovered the plot; and Prussia, to satisfy France, had to banish Stein and two other noblemen, the Prince de Wittgenstein and Count Hardenberg, who had joined him in it. But the Union was not dissolved; it only concealed itself more strictly than before in the masonic brotherhood. During Stein's banishment also the cause was taken up by Jahn, Professor at the Berlin College, who, knowing the beneficial influence of bodily exercise, in 1811 founded a gymnasium, the first of the kind in Germany, which was frequented by the flower of the youth of Berlin, and the members of which were known as *Turner*, an appellation which is now familiar even to Englishmen. These *Turner* seemed naturally called upon to enter into the Union of Virtue; and Jahn thought the moment fast approaching, when the rising against the oppressor was to take place. Among his coadjutors were the poet Arndt, the enthusiastic Schill, who with 400 hussars expected in 1809 to rouse Westphalia and overthrow Jerome Bonaparte; Döremberg,

the Larochejacquelin of Germany, and several
others.   Stein, in the meanwhile, continued at the
court of St. Petersburg the work on account of
which he had been exiled.   The Russian Court
made much of Stein, as a man who might be useful
on certain occasions.   He was especially protected
by the mother of the emperor, in whom he had en-
kindled the same hatred he himself entertained
against France.   He kept up his friendship with the
Berlin patricians, and had his agents in the court of
Prussia, who procured him and Jahn adherents of
note, such as General Blücher.   Still there was at
the Prussian Court a party opposed to the *Tugendbund,* whose chiefs were General Bulow and Schuck-
mann, who preferred peace to the dignity of their
country—who, though no friends to Napoleon, were
indifferent to the public welfare.   A party quite
favourable to the Union of Virtue was that headed
by Baron Nostitz, who formed the society of the
" Knights of the Queen of Prussia," to defend and
avenge that princess, who considered herself to have
been calumniated by Napoleon.   This party was
anxious to wipe away the disgrace of the battle of
Jena, so injurious to the fate, and still more to the
honour, of Prussia; and therefore it naturally made
common cause with the Tugendbund, which aimed
at the same object, the expulsion of the French.

407. *Divisions among Members of Tugendbund.*—
The bases of the organization of the Tugendbund

had been laid in 1807, at the assembly at Königs-berg, where some of the most noted patriots were present—Stein, Stadion, Blücher, Jahn. The asso-ciation deliberated on the means of reviving the energy and courage of the people, arranging the insurrectionary scheme, and succouring the citizens injured by foreign occupation. A man who ac-quired great influence at the time was Justus Grüner. Still there was not sufficient unanimity in the counsels of the association, and an Austrian party began to be formed, which proposed the re-establishment of the German empire, with the Arch-Duke Charles at its head; but the opposition to this scheme came from the side from which it was least to be expected, from the Arch-Duke himself. Some proposed a northern and a southern state; but the many small courts and provincial interests strongly opposed this proposal. Others wanted a republic, which, however, met with very little favour.

408. *Activity of the Tugendbund.* — One of the first acts of the Union of Virtue was to send auxiliary corps to assist the Russians in the cam-paign of 1813. Prussia having, by the course of events, been compelled to abandon its temporizing policy, Greisenau, Scharnhorst, and Grollmann em-braced the military plan of the Tugendbund. A levy *en masse* was ordered. The conduct of these patriots is matter of history. But, like other na-tions, they fought against Napoleon to impose on

their country a more tyrannical government than that of the foreigner had ever been. They fought as men only fight for a great cause, and those who died fancied they saw the dawn of German freedom. But those who survived saw how much they were deceived. The *Tugendbund*, betrayed in its expectations, was dissolved; but its members increased the ranks of other societies already existing, or about to be formed. The "Black Knights," headed by Jahn, continued to exist after the war, as did " The Knights of the Queen of Prussia." Dr. Lang placed himself at the head of the " Concordists," a sect founded in imitation of similar societies already existing in the German universities. A more important association was that of the " German Union" (*Deutscher Bund*), founded in 1810, whose object was the promotion of representative institutions in the various German States. The Westphalian government was the first to discover the existence of this society. Its seal was a lion reposing beside the tree of liberty, surmounted by the Phrygian cap. All these societies were in correspondence with each other, and peacefully divided the territory among themselves; whilst the German Union, true to its name, knew no other limits than those of the German confederation. Dr. Jahn was active in Prussia, Dr. Lang in the north, and Baron Nostitz in the south. This latter, by means of a famous actress of Prague, Madame Brode, won over a Hessian prince, who did not disdain the office of grand master.

409. *Hostility of Governments against Tugendbund.*—After the downfal of Napoleon the German governments, though not venturing openly to attack the Tugendbund, yet sought to suppress it. They assailed it in pamphlets written by men secretly in the pay of Prussia. One of these, Councillor Schmalz, so libelled it as to draw forth indignant replies from Niebuhr and Schleiermacher. What the Germans could least forgive was the scurrilous manner in which Schmalz had calumniated Arndt, the " holy." Schmalz had to fight several duels, and even the favour of the Court of Prussia could not protect him from personal outrages. The king then thought it fit to interfere. He published an ordinance in which he commanded the dispute to cease ; admitted that he had favoured the " literary " society known as the Tugendbund during the days when the country had need of its assistance, but declared that in times of peace secret societies could not be beneficial, but might do a great deal of harm, and therefore forbade their continuance. The action of the government, however, did not suppress the secret societies, though it compelled them to change their names. The Tugendbund was revived in the *Burschenschaft,* or associations of students of the universities, where they introduced gymnastics and martial exercises. Their central committee was in

Prussia; and sub-committees existed at Halle, Leipsic, Jena, Göttingen, Erlangen, Würzburg, Heidelberg, Tübingen, and Freiburg. Germany was divided into ten circles, and there were two kinds of assemblies, preparatory and secret. The liberation and independence of Germany was the subject discussed in the latter; and, Russia being considered as the greatest opponent of their patriotic aspirations, the members directed their operations especially against Russian influences. It was the hatred against Russia that put the dagger into the hand of Charles Louis Sand, the student of Jena, who stabbed Kotzebue, who had written against the German societies, of which there was a considerable number. This murder led to a stricter surveillance of the universities on the part of governments, and secret societies were rigorously prohibited under severe penalties; the Prussian government, especially, being most severe, and prosecuting some of the most distinguished professors for their political opinions. The *Burschenschaft* was broken up, and its objects frustrated, to be revived between 1830-33, to end with a similar failure. Strange, that Prussia, which opposed itself most to the society and its aims, should have reaped all the benefit of these early efforts!

IV.

IRISH SOCIETIES.

410.

HE White-boys.—Ireland, helpless against misery and superstition, misled by hatred, formed sects to fight not so much the evil as the supposed authors of the evil. She would have succeeded better, had she demanded of her sects the strength of economy and the virtue of providence. The first secret society of Ireland, recorded in public documents, dates from 1761, in which year the situation of the peasants, always bad, had become unbearable. They were deprived of the right of free pasture, and the proprietors began to enclose the commons. Fiscal oppression also became very great. Reduced to despair, the conspirators had recourse to reprisals, and to make these with more security, formed the secret society of the " White-boys," so called, because in the hope of disguising themselves, they wore over their clothes a white shirt, like the *Camisards* of the

Cevennes. They also called themselves "Levellers," because their object was to level to the ground the fences of the detested enclosures. In November, 1761, they spread through Munster, committing all kinds of excesses during the next four and twenty years.

411. *Right-boys and Oak-boys.*—In 1787 the above society disappeared to make room for the "Right-boys," who by legal means aimed at obtaining the reduction of imposts; higher wages, the abolition of degrading personal services, and the erection of a Roman Catholic church for every Protestant church in the island. Though the society was guilty of some reprehensible acts against Protestant pastors, it yet, as a rule, remained within the limits of legal opposition. The vicious administration introduced into Ireland after the rising of 1788, the burden of which was chiefly felt by the Roman Catholics, could not but prove injurious to the Protestants also. The inhabitants, whether Catholic or Protestant, were subject to objectionable personal service—hence petitions rejected by the haughty rulers, tumults quenched in blood, whole populations conquered by fear, but not subdued, and ready to break forth into insurrection when it was least expected. Therefore the Protestants also formed societies for their security, taking for their emblem the oak-leaf, whence they were known as the "Oak-boys." Their chief object was to lessen the power and imposts of the clergy. Established in 1764, the society made

rapid progress, especially in the province of Ulster, where it had been founded. Unable to obtain legally what it aimed at, it had recourse to arms, but was defeated by the royal troops of England, and dissolved.

412. *Hearts-of-Steel, Threshers, Break-of-Day-Boys, Defenders, United Irishmen, Ribbonmen.*— Many tenants of the Marquis of Donegal having about eight years after been ejected from their farms, they formed themselves into a society called " Hearts-of-Steel," thereby to indicate the perseverance with which they intended to pursue their revenge against those who had succeeded them on the land, by murdering them, burning their farms, and destroying their harvests. They were not suppressed till 1773, when thousands of the affiliated fled to America, where they entered the ranks of the revolted colonists. The legislative union of Ireland with England in 1800 did not at first benefit the former country much. New secret societies were formed, the most important of which was that of the " Threshers," whose primary object was the reduction of the exorbitant dues claimed by the clergy of both persuasions. The government again was obliged to interfere, but without much success ; time did more to heal the wounds inflicted by these endless important disturbances. Political and religious animosities were further sources of conspiracy. Two societies of almost the same nature

were formed about 1785. The first was composed of Protestants, the "Break-of-day-boys," who at dawn committed all sorts of excesses against the wretched Roman Catholics, burning their huts, and destroying their agricultural implements and produce. The Roman Catholics in return formed themselves into a society of "Defenders," and from defence, as was natural, proceeded to aggression. During the revolt of 1798 the Defenders combined with the "United Irishmen," who had initiated the movement. The United Irish were defeated, but the society was nevertheless not dispersed. Its members still continued to hold secret meetings, and to re-appear in the political arena under the denomination of "Ribbonmen," so named because they recognized each other by certain ribbons.

413. *Saint Patrick Boys.*—These seem to have issued from the ranks of the Ribbonmen. Their statutes were discovered and published in 1833. Their oath was :—" I swear to have my right hand cut off, or to be nailed to the door of the prison at Armagh, rather than deceive or betray a brother; to persevere in the cause to which I deliberately devote myself; to pardon neither sex nor age, should it be in the way of my vengeance against the Orangemen." The brethren recognized each other by dialogues. "Here is a fine day!"—"A finer one is to come."—"The road is very bad."—"It shall

be repaired."—" What with ?"—" With the bones of Protestants."—What is your profession of faith ?"—" The discomfiture of the Philistines."—" How long is your stick ?"—" Long enough to reach my enemies."—" To what trunk does the wood belong?"—" To a French trunk, that blooms in America, and whose leaves shall shelter the sons of Erin." Their aim was chiefly the redress of agrarian and social grievances.

414. *The Orangemen.* — This society, against which the St. Patrick Boys swore such terrible vengeance, was a Protestant Society. Many farms, taken from Roman Catholics, having fallen into the hands of Protestants, these latter were, as we have seen (411), exposed to the attacks of the former. The Protestants in self-defence formed themselves into a society, taking the name of " Orangemen," to indicate their Protestant character and principles. Their first regular meeting was held on the 21st September, 1795, at the obscure village of Loughgall, which was attended by deputies of the Break-of-Day Boys (412), and constituted into a grand lodge, authorized to found minor lodges. At first the lodges were composed entirely of men from the lower ranks; but soon the higher classes began to seek initiation, and the society spread over the whole island, and also into England, and especially into the manufacturing districts. A grand lodge was established at Manchester, which was afterwards

transferred to London, and its grand master was no less a person than the Duke of York. At the death of that prince, which occurred in 1821, the Duke of Cumberland, afterwards King of Hanover, succeeded him—both of them men to have the interests of religion confided to them! In 1835 the Irish statutes, having been revised, were made public. The society bound its members over to defend the royal family, so long as it remained faithful to Protestant principles. In the former statutes there were obligations also to abjure the supremacy of the Court of Rome and the dogma of transubstantiation; and although in the modern statutes these were omitted, others of the same tendency were substituted, the society declaring that its object was the preservation of the religion established by law, the Protestant succession of the crown, and the protection of the lives and property of the affiliated. To concede something to the spirit of the age it proclaimed itself theoretically the friend of religious toleration; but facts have shown this, as in most similar cases, to be a mere illusion. From England the sect spread into Scotland, the colonies, Upper and Lower Canada, where it reckoned 12,000 members; and into the army, with some fifty lodges. In the United States the society has latterly been showing its toleration! Its political action is well known; it endeavours to influence parliamentary elections, supporting the Whigs. The efforts of the British

House of Commons to suppress it have hitherto been ineffectual.

Other Irish societies, having for their chief object the redress of agrarian and religious grievances, were the " Corders," in East and West Meath ; the " Shanavests " and " Caravats " in Tipperary, Kilkenny, Cork, and Limerick.

V.

FENIANS.

415.

ORIGIN and Organization of Fenianism.—
The founders of Fenianism were two of
the Irish exiles of 1848, Colonel John
O'Mahoney and Michael Doheny, the
latter one of the most talented and dangerous members of the Young Ireland party, and a fervent ad-
mirer of John Mitchell. O'Mahoney belonged to one
of the oldest families in Munster, but becoming implicated in Smith O'Brien's machinations and failure,
he made his escape to France, and thence to America,
where in conjunction with Doheny and General
Corcoran he set the Fenian Brotherhood afloat. It
was at first a semi-secret association; its meetings
were secret, and though its chief officers were publicly known as such, the operations of the Brotherhood were hidden from the public view. It rapidly
increased in numbers, spreading through every
state of the American Union, through Canada and

the British Provinces. But in November, 1863, the Fenian organization assumed a new character. A grand national convention of delegates met at Chicago, and avowed the object of the Brotherhood, namely, the separation of Ireland from England, and the establishment of an Irish republic, the same changes being first to be effected in Canada. Another grand convention was held in 1864 at Cincinnati, the delegates at which represented some 250,000 members, each of which members was called upon for a contribution of five dollars, and this call, it is said, was promptly responded to. Indeed, the reader will presently see that the leaders of the movement were never short of money, whatever the dupes were. One of the resolutions passed at Cincinnati was that " the next convention should be held on Irish soil." About the same time a Fenian Sisterhood was established, and the ladies were not inactive; for in two months from their associating they returned upwards of £200,000 sterling to the Fenian exchequer for the purpose of purchasing arms and other war material. At that period the Fenians confidently relied on the assistance of the American Government. The New York press rather favoured this notion. In Ireland the Brotherhood never attained to the dimensions it reached in the United States, and without the assistance of the latter could do nothing. Still the Irish, as well as the American Fenian association, had its chiefs, officers both civil and military, its common fund and financial agencies, its secret oaths, pass-words, and emblems, its laws and penalties, its concealed stores of arms, its nightly drills, its correspondents and agents, its journals, and even its popular songs and ballads. But traitors soon set to work to destroy the organization from within. Thus the Head Centre O' Mahoney, who was in receipt of an official salary of 2,000 dollars, is thus spoken of in the Official Report of the Investigating Committee of the Fenian Brotherhood of America (1866) :—

" After a careful examination of the affairs of the Brotherhood your Committee finds in almost every instance the cause of Ireland made subservient to individual gain; men who were lauded as patriots sought every opportunity to plunder the treasury of the Brotherhood, but legalized their attacks by securing the endorsement of John O'Mahoney. . . . In John O'Mahoney's integrity the confidence of the Brotherhood was boundless, and the betrayal of that confidence, whether through incapacity or premeditation, is not a question for us to determine. . . . . Sufficient that he has proved recreant to the trust. . . . . Never in the history of the Irish people did they repose so much confidence in their leaders ; never before were they so basely deceived and treacherously dealt with. In fact, the Moffat mansion (the head-quarters of the American Fenians), was not only an almshouse for pauper officials and hungry adventurers, but a general telegraph office for the Canadian authorities, and Sir Frederick Bruce, the British minister at Washington. These paid patriots and professional martyrs, not satisfied with emptying our treasury, connived at posting the English authorities in advance of our movements."

From this Report it farther appears that in 1866 there was in the Fenian Treasury in the States a sum of 185,000 dollars; that the expenses of the Moffat mansion and the parasites who flocked thither in three months amounted to 104,000 dollars; and that Stephens, the Irish Head Centre in the same space of time received from America, in money sent to Paris, the sum of upwards of 106,000 dollars, though John O'Mahoney in many of his letters expressed the greatest mistrust of Stephens. He no doubt looked upon the latter as the more clever and daring rogue, who materially diminished his own share of the spoil. Stephens' career in Ireland is sufficiently well known, and there is scarcely any doubt that whilst he was leading his miserable associates to their ruin, he acted as spy upon them, and that there existed some understanding between him and the English authorities. How else can we explain his living for nearly two months in the neighbourhood of Dublin, in a house magnificently furnished, whilst he took no precautions to conceal himself, and yet escaped the vigilance of the police for so long a time? His conduct when at last apprehended, his bravado in the police-court and final escape from prison, all point to the same conclusion. The only other person of note among the Fenians was John Mitchell, who had been implicated in the troubles of 1848, was transported, escaped, and made his way to the United States. During the civil war which raged in that country he was a supporter of the Southern cause, was taken prisoner by the North, but liberated by the President at the request of the Fenians in America.

The Fenian agitation also spread into England. Meetings were held in various towns, especially at Liverpool, where men of considerable means were found to support the Fenian objects and organization; and on one occasion as much as £200 was collected in a few minutes in the room where a meeting was held. But disputes about the money thus collected were ever arising. The man who acted as treasurer to the Liverpool Centre, when accused of plundering his brethren, snapped his fingers at them, and declared that if they bothered him about the money, he would give evidence against them and have the whole lot hanged. The Fenians, to raise money, issued bonds to be redeemed by the future Irish Republic, of one of which the following is a facsimile:—

Harp.	£1	Goddess of Liberty.	£1	Shamrock.

Ninety days after the establishment of

THE IRISH REPUBLIC

Redeemable by _____ { Board of
           _____ { Finance.

Sunburst.	

416. *Origin of Name.*—Irish tradition says that the Fenians were an ancient militia employed on home service for protecting the coasts from invasion. Each of the four provinces had its band, that of Leinster, to which Fionn and his family belonged, being at the head of the others. This Fionn is the Fingal of MacPherson, and the leaders of the movement no doubt saw an advantage in connecting their party with the historical and traditionary glories of Ireland. But the Fenians were not confined to Erin.

In the ancient poem on the battle of Gabhra we read of "the bards of the Fians of Alban," Alban being the old name of Scotland; and also that "the Fians of Lochlan were powerful." Now Lochlan was an ancient name for Germany north of the Rhine, but when the Norwegian and Danish pirates appeared in the ninth century, they were called Lochlanaels, and the name of Lochlan was transferred to Norway and Denmark. Hence it has been argued that the Fenians were not a militia of Gaels, but that they were a distinct Celtic race.

417. *Fenian Litany.*—From the Patriotic Litany of Saint Lawrence O'Toole, published for the use of the Fenian Brotherhood, the following extracts may suffice :—

" Call to thine aid, O most liberty-loving O'Toole, those Christian auxiliaries of power and glory—the soul-inspiring cannon, the meek and faithful musket, the pious rifle, and the conscience-examining pike, which, tempered by a martyr's faith, a Fenian's hope, and a rebel's charity, will triumph over the devil, and restore to us our own in our own land for ever. Amen.

O'Toole hear us.

From English civilization,
From British law and order,
From Anglo-Saxon cant and
    freedom,
From the hest of the English
    Queen,
From Rule Britannia,   *O'Toole deliver us !*
From the cloven hoof,
From the necessity of annual
    rebellion,
From billeted soldiery,
From a pious church establish-
    ment,

From the slavery of praying
   for crowned heads,
From royal anniversaries,
From mock trials,
From all other things purely
   English,

O'Toole deliver us!

Fenianism the salvation of our race!

Record it above, O'Toole.

Fenianism to be stamped out like the cattle plague!

We will prove them false prophets, O'Toole.

Ireland reduced to obedience,
Ireland loyal to the crown,
Ireland pacified with conces-
   sions,
Ireland to recruit the British
   army,
Ireland not united in effort,

It is a falsehood, O'Toole.

Ireland never again to be dragged at the tail of any other nation!

Proclaim it on high, O'Toole.

418. *Events.*—In speaking of Stephens it was mentioned that he was a spy on the Fenians, but he was not the only informer that betrayed his confederates to the English Government; which latter, in consequence of "information thus received," made its first descent on the Brotherhood in 1865, at the office of the *Irish People*, and captured some of the leading Fenians. Shortly after, it seized Stephens,

who, however, was allowed to make his escape from
Richmond Prison, where he had been confined in
the night of November 24 of the above year.
Further arrests took place in other parts of Ireland,
and also at Liverpool, Manchester, and other English
towns. The prisoners were indicted for treason-
felony, and sentenced to various degrees of punishment. Various raids into Canada, and the attempt
on Chester Castle, all ending in failure, next showed
that Fenianism was still alive. But it was more prominently again brought before the public by the attack at Manchester, in September, 1867, on the police
van conveying two leaders of the Fenian conspiracy,
Kelly and Deasey, to the city prison, who were
enabled to make their escape, whilst Serjeant Brett
was shot dead by William O'Meara Allen, who was
hanged for the deed. A still more atrocious and
fatal Fenian attempt was that made on the Clerkenwell House of Detention, with a view of liberating
two Fenian prisoners, Burke and Casey, when a
great length of the outer wall of the prison was
blown up by gunpowder, which also destroyed a
whole row of houses opposite, killed several persons,
and wounded and maimed a great number. On
that occasion again government had received information of the intended attempt by traitors in the
camp, but strangely enough failed to take proper
precautionary measures. On December 24, 1867,
the Fenians made an attack on the Martello Tower

at Fota, near Queenstown, co. Cork, and carried
off a quantity of arms and ammunition; and their
latest exploit was another Canadian raid, when they
crossed the border at Pembina, and seized the
Canadian Custom House and Hudson's Bay post.
They were, however, attacked and dispersed by
American troops, and General O'Neil was made
prisoner. This raid was carried out totally independently of the new Irish Fenian confederation, of
which O'Donovan Rossa was the moving spirit; and
the Irish papers therefore poohpoohed the account of
this *fiasco* altogether, or merely gave the telegrams,
denying that the enterprise had any connection with
Fenianism.   There is, in fact, scarcely any doubt,
that the Fenian Brotherhood is breaking up;
O' Donovan Rossa has retired from the " Directory"
of the confederation and gone into the wine trade.
The Fenians themselves have denounced the notorious Stephens, who reappeared in America, as a
"traitor" and government informer; and though
the acquittal of Kelly for the murder of head-con-
stable Talbot would seem to point to a strong
sympathy still surviving amongst the Irish people
with Fenianism, the jury perhaps could give no
other verdict than the one they arrived at, the
prosecution having been altogether mismanaged by
the government.

419. *Comic Aspects of Fenianism.*—The account of
the Fenian movement is necessarily dull; the reader

may therefore be pleased to see one or two extracts from a comic history of it, taken from an American work, entitled, "The New Gospel of Peace according to St. Benjamin" (1867). The author writes: —"About those days there arose certain men, Padhees, calling themselves Phainyans, who conspired together to wrest the' isle of Ouldairin from the queen of the land of Jonbool. Now it was from the isle of Ouldairin that the Padhees came into the land of Unculpsalm. . . . Although the Padhees never had established government or administered laws in Ouldairin, they diligently sought instead thereof to have shyndees therein, first with the men who sought to establish a government for them; but if not with them, then with each other. . . . Now the Padhees in the land of Unculpsalm said one to another, Are we not in the land of Unculpsalm, where the power of Jonbool cannot touch us, and we are many and receive money; let us therefore conspire to make a great shyndee in the isle of Ouldairin. . . . And they took a large upper room 'and they placed men at the outside of the outer door, clad in raiment of green and gold, and having drawn swords in their hands. For they said, How shall men know that we are conspiring secretly, unless we set a guard over ourselves? And they chose a chief man to rule them, and they called him the Hid-Sinter, which, being interpreted, is the top-middle; for, in the tongue of the Padhees,

hid is top, and *sinter* is middle. . . . And it came
to pass that after many days the Hid-Sinter sent
out tax-gatherers, and they went among the Padhees, and chiefly among the Bihdees throughout
the city of Gotham, and the other cities in the land
of Unculpsalm, and they gathered tribute, . . . and
the sum thereof was great, even hundreds of thousands of pieces of silver. Then the Hid-Sinter and
his chief officers took unto themselves a great house
and spacious in the city of Gotham . . . and fared
sumptuously therein, and poured out drink-offerings
night and day unto the isle of Ouldairin. And
they set up a government therein, which they called
the government of Ouldairin, and chose unto themselves certain lawgivers, which they called the Sinnit.
. . . Now it came to pass when certain of the Padhees, Phainyans, saw that the Hid-Sinter and his
chief officers . . . fared sumptuously every day . . .
and lived as if all their kinsfolk were dying day by
day, and there was a ouaic without end, that their
souls were moved with envy, and they said each
within his own heart, Why should I not live in a
great house and fare sumptuously? But unto each
other and unto the world they said:—Behold, the
Hid-Sinter and his officers do not govern Ouldairin
righteously, and they waste the substance of the
people. Let us therefore declare their government to be at an end, and let us set up a new
government, with a new Hid-Sinter, and a new

Sinnit, even ourselves. And they did so. And they declared that the first Hid-Sinter was no longer Hid-Sinter, but that their Hid-Sinter was the real Hid-Sinter, . . . and moreover they especially declared that tribute money should no more be paid to the first Hid-Sinter, but unto theirs. But the first Hid-Sinter and his officers would not be set at nought. . . . and so it came to pass that there were three governments for the isle of Ould-airin; one in the land of Jonbool, and two in the city of Gotham in the land of Unculpsalm. But when the Phainyans gathered unto themselves men, Padhees, in the island of Ouldairin, who went about there in the night-time, with swords and with spears and with staves, the governors sent there by the queen of Jonbool took those men and cast some of them into prison, and banished others into a far country," &c.

VI.

THE COMMUNISTS.

420.

ECRET *Societies in Spain.*—Even before the French Revolution there existed in Spain secret societies, some averse to monarchical government, others in favour of clerocracy. Among the latter may be mentioned the " Concessionists," who carried their zeal for Ferdinand VII. and their tenderness for the Church to such a degree as to desire the return of the blessed times of the Holy Inquisition. They also sought to get hold of the management of public affairs to turn them to their own profit; and the dismal administration of the Bourbons shows that they partly succeeded. Probably from this association arose that of the " Defenders of the Faith," Jesuits in disguise, who in 1820 spread themselves over Spain, taking care of the throne and altar, and still more of themselves. During the reign of Ferdinand VII. also arose the " Realists," who, to

benefit themselves, encouraged the king in his reactionary policy.

421. *Freemasonry in Spain.*—After the French
invasion of 1809, Freemasonry was restored in the
Peninsula, and a Grand Orient established at Madrid;
but it confined itself to works of popular education
and charity, entirely eschewing politics. The fall
of Joseph and the restoration again put an end
to these well-meant efforts. In 1816, some of the
officers and soldiers, returned from French prisons,
joined and formed independent lodges, establishing
a Grand Orient at Madrid, very secret, and in correspondence with the few French lodges that meddled
with politics. Among the latter is remembered the
lodge of the "Sectaries of Zoroaster," which initiated
several Spanish officers residing in Paris, among
others Captain Quezada, who afterwards favoured
the escape of the patriot Mina. The revolution of
the island of Leon was the work of restored Spanish
Masonry, which had long prepared for it under the
direction of Quiroga, Riego, and five members of
the Cortes.

422. *The Communists.*—After the brief victory,
badly concealed jealousies broke forth; many of the
brethren seceded and formed a new society, the
" Confederation of the Communists" (*Comuneros*),
which name was derived from that memorable
epoch of Spanish history when Charles V. attempted
to destroy the ancient liberties, and thus provoked

the revolution of the Commons in 1520, which was
headed by John Padilla, and afterwards by his
heroic wife, Maria Pacheco. In the battle of Villa-
lar the Communists were defeated and scattered,
and the revolution was doomed. The new Communists, reviving these memories, declared their
intentions, which could not but be agreeable to
Young Spain; nearly sixty thousand members
joined the Society. Their meetings were called
torres (towers), and presided over by a " Grand
Castellan." The scope of the society was to promote by all means in its power the freedom of
mankind; to defend in every way the rights of the
Spanish people against the abuses and encroach-
ments of royal and priestly power; and to succour
the needy, especially those belonging to the society.
On being initiated the candidate was first led into
the " hall of arms," where he was told of the obligations and duties he was about to undertake. His
eyes having been bandaged he was conducted to
another room, where, after he had declared that he
wished to be admitted into the confederation, a
member acting as sentinel exclaimed:—"Let him
advance, I will escort him to the guard-house of the
castle." Then there was imitated with great noise
the lowering of a drawbridge, and the raising of a
portcullis; the candidate was then led into the
guard-room, unbandaged, and left alone. The walls
were covered with arms and trophies, and with

patriotic and martial inscriptions. Being at last admitted into the presence of the governor, the candidate was thus addressed :—" You stand now under the shield of our chief Padilla ; repeat with all the fervour you are capable of the oath I am about to dictate to you." By this oath, the candidate bound himself to fight for constitutional liberty, and to avenge every wrong done to his country. The new knight then covered himself with the shield of Padilla, the knights present pointed their swords at it, and the governor continued :—" The shield of our chief Padilla will cover you from every danger, will save your life and honour ; but if you violate your oath this shield shall be removed, and these swords buried in your breast." Both the Masons and Communists sought to gain possession of superior political influence. The former, having more experience, prevailed in the elections and formed the ministry. Hence a contest that agitated the country and injured the cause of liberty. In 1832, the Communists endeavoured to overthrow the Freemasons, but unsuccessfully. Still Masons and Communists combined to oppose the reactionary party. They also succeeded in suppressing Carbonarism, which had been introduced into Spain by some refugee Italians. These societies, in fact, though professing patriotic views, were nothing but egotistical cliques, bent on their own aggrandisement. How little they were guided by fixed principles is shown by their conduct in Spanish America. In Brazil they placed on the throne Don Pedro, and in Mexico they established a republican form of government, just as it best suited their own private interests. But such is the practice of most patriots.

VII.

INTERNATIONAL AND COMMUNE.

423.

*I*NTRODUCTORY *Remarks*. — There exists an association of working—or rather, *talking*—men, pretending to have for its object the uniting in one fraternal bond the workers of all countries, and the advocating of the interests of labour, and those only. Though it protests against being a secret society, it yet indulges in such underhand dealings, insidiously endeavouring to work mischief between employers and employed, and aiming at the subversion of the existing order of things, that it deserves to be denounced with all the societies professedly secret. In this country its influence is scarcely 'felt, because the English workmen that join it are numerically few—according to the statement of the Secretary of the International himself, the society counts only about 8,000 English members—and these, with here and there an exception, belong to the most worthless portion of the working classes. It is chiefly the idle and dissipated or unskilled artizan that thinks his position is to be improved by others and not by himself. To hear the interested demagogues and paid agitators of the " International," the working classes would seem to be exceptionally oppressed, and to labour under disadvantages greater than any that weigh upon other sections of the community. Yet no other class is so much protected by the legislature, and none, except the paupers, pay less towards the general expenses of the country in direct or indirect taxation. The wages a skilled artizan can earn are higher than the remuneration obtainable by thousands of men who have enjoyed an university education, or sunk money in some professional apprenticeship; whilst he is free from the burden incident to maintaining a certain social status. His hours of labour are such as to leave him plenty of leisure for enjoyment, especially in this country; and as regards extra holidays, he is on the whole pretty liberally dealt with, especially by the large employers of labour, the capitalists, against whom the street-spouters, who for their own advantage get up public demonstrations, are always inveighing in a manner which would be simply ridiculous were it not mischievous. But then if they did not constantly attempt to render the workman dissatisfied with his lot, their occupation would be gone. And so, as the doctors who, for want of patients, get up hospitals for the cure of particular diseases, try to persuade every man they come in contact with, that he is suffering from some such disease; so these agitators endeavour to talk the workman into the delusion that he is the most unfortunate and most oppressed individual under the sun. To wish to act for oneself and work out one's own salvation is no doubt very praiseworthy; but workmen ought to bear in mind that they may be the tools of ambitious men in their own class, who look upon and use them as such for their own purposes, men who want to be generals commanding soldiers. But the soldiers of the International are not worth much. Those workmen who are not satisfied with adhering to the statutes of the society in order to get rid of troublesome appeals, and to avoid being molested by their comrades, but who fervently embrace its principles and count upon their success, usually are the most idle, the least saving, the least sober. The fanatics of the society, those who ought to form its principal strength, are formed, not by the *élite*, but by the scum of the working classes. The chiefs are not much better. The more intelligent and honest founders of the society have gradually withdrawn from it in disgust. As to their successors, they have constantly shown themselves incapable and dishonest. They inspire no feeling but that of contempt. And even those endowed with a little intelligence, on purpose to maintain themselves at the head of the incongruous mass they direct, have frequently been compelled to submit to its influence—hence many of the egregious blunders committed by them both before, and still more after, March 18, 1871. In the party of demagogues the head is most frequently led by the tail. The saying, "You know I must follow them, since I am their leader," may with great appropriateness be used by the leaders of the International. A socialistic school recognised the necessity of the concurrence of three elements in every enterprise—work, capital and talent. The International recruits its members among workers that dislike work; it declares capital infamous and proscribes it; as to talent it has shown that its chiefs are altogether destitute of it. It may perhaps engage us in a few more sanguinary conflicts, but we may be quite sure that never in any part of the world will it win a decisive and lasting victory. It is certain that the majority of French, English, German, Italian, Spanish, and Russian workmen look upon the principles of the International as false, unjust, immoral, and, what is much more to the purpose, impracticable.

424. *Socialistic Schemes.*—Schemes for the regeneration of mankind have been hatched in every age, from Plato and his Republic down to Louis Blanc's *Organisation du Travail*, and the International. Many communistic movements took place

in the sixteenth century, and the brief history of the Anabaptist kingdom of Munster presents striking resemblances with that of the recent Commune of Paris. Babeuf and the Conspiracy of the Equals remind us of the demagogues who lately filled Paris with blood and fire. The *collegia opificum* of Rome, the guilds of France and Germany, the trades-corporations, the compagnonnage—all these were the fore-runners of modern trade-unions and the International. The systems of Saint-Simon, Fourier, Cabet, Louis Blanc, and Owen, also had their day. That of Louis Blanc seemed the most feasible, but what has been its success? Of the 180 workmen's associations formed according to his system there were, in 1867, only ten still in existence; and their gains during the years of their activity bear no comparison to the wages earned during the same period by workmen giving their time to capitalists. Co-operative societies formed by artisans never did and never can pay. When an association is formed for the manufacture and sale of certain products, it not only wants hands to work, but a head to direct—a manager, who, being necessarily a man of superior parts, is also entitled to superior rank and superior pay. But when workmen, striving after an equality which is unattainable, assign the post of manager to a man who possesses none of the superior qualifications, the affairs of the association soon go wrong;

if he be a man of greater capacity, he soon contrives to acquire an influence which renders him the virtual master of his fellow-labourers. It has also frequently happened that an·incapable or dishonest manager has all at once disappeared with the strong box of the association. Sometimes he, as by a *coup d'état*, seizes the sovereign power. Thus the association of arm-chair makers of Paris, founded in 1848 with 400 members, and re-constructed in 1849 with only twenty associates, underwent many other vicissitudes, until the manager, M. Antoine, made himself absolute master of it. " Well," he said to M. Huber, a German, who travelled through France and England to study the subject of co-operation,— " well, yes, I too have achieved my small *coup d'état*. And why should I not have done it, since *coups d'état* answer so well ?" This manager, however, disappeared a few years after, under circumstances which caused the association to draw very long faces indeed. There is, in fact, no authenticated record of any co-operative association of workmen whose success has been such as to encourage imitation. But coalitions of workmen have been more success-ful. Whilst co-operation means peace and produc-tion, coalition means war and destruction. Where-fore in some countries, and especially in France, very stringent laws have at various times been enacted against workmen forming coalitions, either on the part of workmen to refuse the work offered by the capitalist, or on the part of employers to lower the workmen's wages. The employers, however, easily evaded the law; and numerous workmen's coalitions formed in France in spite of it, gave constant occupation to the tribunals. In this country no law has been passed against trade-unions, and therefore they flourish here, and have led to deplorable events, such as the Sheffield outrages, which, for diabolical fury, deserve to be placed side by side with the doings of the Commune. The reader will probably remember the fact that men who had belonged to the Sheffield trade-unions, but withdrew from them, were assassinated, their houses blown up, and every imaginable kind of tyranny and persecution practised upon them for the space of some fifteen years. Still, as the majority of the Parisian workmen were innocent of the crimes of the Commune, so the trade-unions were not answerable for the doings of a restricted number of their members. But these trade-unions are still to be condemned, because they are the instigators and upholders of strikes, the greatest curse, not on the hated capitalist, but on the poor workman. Now the International is a combination of trade-unions, with the additional poison of Communism diffused throughout its system.

425. *History of the International.*—The first attempt at an international society was made by a small number of German workmen in London, who

had been expelled from France in 1839 for taking part in the *émeute* in Paris. Its members consisted of Germans, Hungarians, Poles, Danes, and Swedes. Of the few English members Ernest Jones was one. The society was on friendly terms with the English Socialists, the Chartists, and the London French Democratic Society. Out of that friendship sprang the Society of the Fraternal Democrats, who were in correspondence with a number of democratic societies in Belgium. In November, 1847, a German Communist Conference was held in London, at which Dr. Karl Marx was present. In the manifesto then put forth it was declared that the aim of the Communists was the overthrow of the rule of the capitalists by the acquisition of political power. The practical measures by which this was to be effected were the abolition of private property in land; the centralization of credit in the hands of the State—the leading agitators of course to be the chiefs of the State—by means of a national bank; the centralization of the means of transport in the hands of the State; national workshops; the reclamation and improvement of land; and the gratuitous education of all the children. But all these fine schemes of amelioration, or rather spoliation, in consequence of the Revolution of February, 1848, ended in smoke; and it was not till the year 1859, when the London builders' dispute arose, that new alliances among the working men were formed.

In 1860, a Trade Unionist, Manhood Suffrage, and Vote by Ballot Association was established, of which G. Odger, a shoemaker, was chairman. As if it had not enough of what might be called legitimate work to do, the association also undertook to agitate in favour of Poland, for which purpose it co-operated with the National League for the Independence of Poland. The London International Exhibition of 1862 induced the French government to assist many French workmen with means to visit that exhibition; "a visit," said the French press, "which will enable our workmen to study the great works of art and industry, remove the leaven of international discord, and replace national jealousies by fraternal emulation." It is impossible to say how far these French workmen studied the works of art and industry exhibited in 1862; but it is quite certain that the old leaven of international discord, which up to that time had not been very formidable, was speedily replaced by a new leaven of social discord, not so virulent at first, it is true, as it subsequently became in the after-days of the International. Many of the original members of this association in fact eventually withdrew from it; as they refused to be identified with its excesses, which had not been planned or foreseen by its founders. On the 5th of August, all the delegates met at a dinner given to them by their English colleagues at Freemasons' Hall, when an address was read which formed, as it were, the foundation-stone of the International. The Imperial Commission that had enabled the French workmen to visit the London Exhibition had no doubt furnished them with return tickets. But several of the artizans made no use of their second halves, since profitable employment in London was found for them by their English brethren, so that they might form connecting links between the workmen of the two countries, The next year a new meeting was found necessary. There was no longer an Exhibition, nor subsidies from the Imperial government to pay travelling expenses. The pretext, however, was found in a demonstration just then made in favour of Poland. Six French delegates, having mulcted their mates in contributions towards the pleasant trip, came over, and the democrats of London and Paris were invited to co-operate in the liberation of Poland, and to form an international working men's alliance. Various meetings were held and all the stale twaddle concerning Poland and the emancipation of the working classes talked over again. A central committee of working men of different countries to have its seat in London —truly England is the political and social dunghill of Europe!—was appointed, and a collection of course followed, which at the most important meeting realized three guineas. A paltry sum after so much talk! The members of the committee, holding its powers by the resolution of the public meeting held on Sept. 28, 1864, at St. Martin's Hall, then declared the International Working Men's Association to be established; and congresses were appointed to be held at different times and places, to decide on the measures to be taken to found the working men's Eldorado. Many societies at first were affiliated, but dissensions soon broke out among them, and many, such as the Italian Working Men's Society, withdrew again. At a meeting held in London, in 1865, the " re-establishment of Poland entire and independent" was again one of the questions discussed. The Paris delegates were for avoiding political questions; but Mr. Odger reminded them that Poland had furnished the occasion for the establishment of the association, and that the Conference must stand by the Polish cause. The infatuation of Mr. Odger's dupes is something astounding! To gratify the vanity of a political agitator, who, knowing very well that his International is a mere bogey, a turnip with a rushlight inside, endeavours to surround it with the halo of a great political scheme and martial glory—it is for this that English workmen, who neither know, nor in fact care for, the affairs of Poland, are to give their money—so little, and according to Mr. Odger himself, earned with such difficulty—robbing their wives and children, that some day it may be trumpeted to the world how Mr. Odger stood forth the champion of Poland! Would not this be "squandering the people's blood and treasure," my worthy shoe-maker? Well, in 1866, a meeting or congress was held at Geneva, where it was decided that an inquiry into the condition of the working classes of all countries should be made respecting rate of wages, hours of labour, &c. This inquiry has not been made as yet; of course not, though the English government has gathered by means of its consular agents, and published by means of blue books, an immense amount of information on the subject. But then it does not talk so grandly about the emancipation of the working classes as Mr. Odger and his partners! And this inquiry on the part of the International was to be a preliminary to practical measures—no wonder that the association has as yet produced nothing practical. At this Geneva Congress a great number of other resolutions were passed, which remain resolutions still. Thus co-operation was to be encouraged; but, as the individual "wages-slaves" could never elaborate it, general social changes were to be effected; the state power was to be transferred from capitalists and landlords to the producers themselves. Re-solutions were also passed in favour of transferring railways and other means of locomotion to the people, and of destroying the monopoly of the great companies "that subject the working classes to arbitrary laws, assailing both the dignity of man and individual liberty." What with parliamentary trains and cheap fares, the working classes can scarcely complain of being arbitrarily oppressed. Perhaps they think their dignity would be enhanced by their riding in first-class carriages at third-class fares. Resolutions were also passed in favour of direct taxation. How this suggestion would be received by the working man has very pleasantly been pointed out by " Punch " or some other comic paper:—" Mrs. Brown (*loq.*)—'Well, Mrs. Jones, my husband says that if they tax him, he will take it out in parish relief.' " The abolition of standing armies and the independence of Poland—Poland again—were also decided on. Both these points are still decided on, and will probably remain at the same interesting stage of progress a little longer !

426. *Objects and Aims of International.*—To sum up what has been proposed at the later congresses :—Quarries, coal and other mines, as well as railways, shall belong to the social collectivity, represented by the state; but by the state regenerated, that will concede them, not, as now, to capitalists, but to associations of workmen. The soil shall be granted to agricultural associations; canals, roads, telegraphs, and forests, shall belong collectively to society. Contracts of lease, or letting, shall be converted into contracts of sale; that is to say, capital shall no longer be entitled to claim interest. If I borrow £1,000 I shall have paid off the debt in twenty years by an annual payment of £50. Such

are the doctrines of this society, whose motto is, *La propriété, c'est le vol.* All these, however, are clothed in very fine words—" economic evolution," " social collectivity," " scientific and rational exploitation," " social liquidation," &c., though now and then one of the members uses less flowery language. Thus, at the Congress of Bâle, held in 1869, Bakounine, a Russian Nihilist, spoke thus without reserve :—" By social liquidation I mean expropriation of all existing proprietors, by the abolition of the political and legal state, which is the sanction and only guarantee of all property as now existing, and of all that is called legal right; and the expropriation, in fact, everywhere, and as much and as quickly as possible, by the force of events and circumstances." There is no reticence here ! No Congress met in 1870, in consequence of the war; but the programme that was to have formed the subject of discussion has been published. The first question was :—On the necessity of abolishing the public debt. The third :—Concerning practical means for converting landed and funded property into social property. The fifth :—Conditions of co-operative production on a national scale. The Belgian Committee proposed as an additional question :—Concerning the practical means for constituting agricultural sections in the International. Thus private property was to be abolished, private enterprise destroyed, and the poison of Communism, with which large towns are now infected, to be diffused throughout the country. What would these men have done, could they, according to their intention, have met in Paris in 1870 ? The pertinacity with which the cause of Poland is sought to be identified with the objects of the International has already been alluded to. Poland seems a mine that can never be exhausted. Thousands of rogues and vagabonds of all countries have fattened, are fattening, and will yet fatten on this carcase, as burntout tradesmen have been known to flourish on the fire by which they lost everything ! The International, moreover, in declaring war to all tyrants, of course sanctifies their destruction; the attempt of the Pole, Berezowski, to shoot the Emperor of Russia, while on a visit to the Emperor Napoleon, on June 6, 1867, was one of the results of the teaching of the International.

427. *The International on the Continent.*—In this country, as we have seen, the International has as yet only had a limited success. It has indeed held public meetings and demonstrations, and led to some insignificant riots, for the occurrence of which our government of course is very much to blame; though no surprise can be felt at its supineness, considering the weakness and pusillanimity it has shown when opposed to, or rather by, the Fenians. There are, indeed, alarmists, who are led astray by the " bounce" of the International, and who thus

invest it with greater importance than intrinsically attaches to it. Thus a Paris paper some time ago contained a letter from a London correspondent which gave an awful picture of the danger threatening this country from the spread of socialistic doctrines. The writer said :—" The whole of this vast empire is permeated by secret societies. The International here holds its meetings almost publicly. It is said that the greater number of the dispossessed princes of India, a good number of officers belonging to the army and navy, as well as members of parliament, and even ministers, are affiliated to it (!). The government is aware of the infernal plan by which, at a given moment, the public buildings of London are to be exposed to the fate which befel so many in Paris. Boats are already waiting on the Thames to receive the treasures of the Bank of England— an easy prey, say the conspirators—as soon as the main artery of the Strand shall have been burnt, and the public buildings, the barracks especially, shall have been blown up, as was three years ago the Clerkenwell prison." If this is not sensational writing, what is ? But perhaps the writer was only joking; and if I thought the leaders of the International possessed any Machiavellian talent, I should say they themselves caused the letter to be written to give the world an exaggerated idea of their power —therein imitating the president of the London Republican Club, who boasts of his power of pulling down the monarchy, as that would be the readiest means of attracting fresh members; for the idea of belonging to a powerful and universally diffused brotherhood exercises a great fascination over the minds of only partially educated men, such as form the bulk of the working classes. But the most nervous old gentleman, residing in one of the quiet by-streets off the Strand, may as yet sleep in peace; the International will not burn that thoroughfare, nor set the Thames on fire.

Abroad, however, its action has been much more marked. It has fomented serious riots in Holland, Belgium, and France; and in the last-named country it has especially stimulated Communism, and supported the Paris Commune in all its atrocities, of which it speaks in the most laudatory terms in its recently published pamphlet, " The Civil War in France" (Truelove, 1871). But even continental workmen have ere this discovered the hollowness of the International. The working engineers of Brussels, instead of receiving during a recent strike 15 francs weekly, as promised, were paid only 6 francs; and having imposed upon the masters an augmentation of 50 per cent. on overtime, the masters, in order to avoid this ruinous tariff, had no work performed after the regular hours. The men, finding themselves losers by this rule, enforced on them by the International, sent in their resignations as members of the society, which they

described as the " Leprosy of Europe," and the
" Company of Millionnaires . . . . on paper." At a
conference held in London the Russian delegate
urged that his country especially offered an excellent
field for the spread of socialist doctrines, and that
the students were quite ripe for revolution. Where-
fore it was decided that a special appeal should be
addressed to the Russian students and workmen.
Truly, Russia has a right to complain of the laxity
of the English government, which allows a set of
wretches openly to conspire in the capital of England
against the peace and security of a friendly state.
Nor are these machinations without result. Among
their fruits may be reckoned the Nihilists, and
another secret society, disguising its Communistic aims under the cloak of religious reformation.
The founder of this sect, who recently made his appearance in the neighbourhood of Tekatarinosloff,
scorned to speak in prose, but delivered his doctrines
in a kind of doggrel, preaching polygamy, the abroga-
tion of all denominational creeds, and utter religious
license, and proclaiming himself the Saviour. But
the Russian police can no doubt by this time give a
very good account of the impostor and his dupes.

428. *How the International Works.*—What pre-
cedes has sufficiently shown with what ardour the
International supports strikes, and the importance
it attaches to their success. The complete history
of the coalitions to which it has given its aid, would

almost form the subject of European history during the last seven or eight years. But the documents for such an account are not yet accessible; still enough is known to prove what has been mentioned on several occasions—that the International seeks to render workmen dissatisfied with their condition, to make them feel as patients whom the International alone can cure. To give an instance. On April 2, 1869, a strike occurred among the puddlers at the ironworks of Cockerill and Co., at Seraing. After some discussion the difficulty was arranged by mutual concessions, and no disturbances took place. On the day of the strike the International received 250 new adherents, whom it accepted on condition that they abstained from all violent manifestations, represented their grievances with moderation, and demanded nothing but what was just. We shall see presently what the International meant by moderation. The men had returned to their work. "For four days," says the *Internationale* of April 18, "the most perfect calm reigned in the workshops, for the proprietors had taken care to remove a detested manager. But on the fifth day he was re-introduced by one of the directors; and immediately all the puddlers struck again, and with them all the other hands." By this account, taken from the official journal of the association, it appears clearly enough what in reality had taken place. The International wanted a strike of the puddlers, but did not at first succeed. The workmen came to an agreement with their masters too soon; but the International had its revenge. The return of the detested manager was only a pretext; for in the account published in the *Réveil* of Seraing, between the first resumption of work and its second interruption, all the grievances of the workmen are fully enumerated, but there is not the least mention of any detested manager. This time however the International succeeded to the whole extent of its wishes. It had in all probability desired and fomented a partial strike, for its interest of course is to have as few mouths to feed as possible. When once the concessions demanded by the hands on strike are extorted from the masters, they are as a rule easily imposed on all the chiefs of the same industry. These tactics are well understood, and are those usually pursued by the association. But in this instance the strike of the puddlers also dragged into its vortex other workmen but little versed in industrial strategy. And so the rest of the hands also went on strike, in spite of the prudent advice of the members of the International, who endeavoured to show them the inconvenience of this measure. Other strikes followed in the same neighbourhood; and the result was that serious riots ensued, the military had to be called in, and two workmen were killed. Out of this circumstance the International of course made capital, declaring the soldiers to be the hired cut-throats of the capitalists, though all they then wanted was to protect their property; for they well remembered the events of Roubaix in 1867, when a mob of workmen destroyed not only the looms and material in seven factories, but also sacked the private houses of two manufacturers, throwing the furniture, beds, and all other property into the street. A more recent instance of the underhand working of the International is detailed in the following letter from Brussels, published in the *Hainault* of Mons. The writer states that a respectable manufacturer of Brussels met a short time since one of the well-known leaders of the International, who asked him if he had seen the *Liberté*, and informed him that it gave a letter to him from his workmen, containing their ultimatum preliminary to a strike. He told him that the letter would reach him next day at the latest. The manufacturer procured a copy of the paper, and to his astonishment read a letter full of exaggerations and misstatements. On reflection he was convinced that his workpeople could never have sought an advance of wages on such absurd and mendacious pretences; and further he esteemed it not an insignificant fact that the letter had appeared in a journal before he had heard anything of it. However, he determined to wait for the letter, which reached him the next day; and he found to his surprise that the names of all his workmen were appended to it. Having read it carefully, he repaired to his factory, when he assembled all the hands and said—" My friends, you have sent me a letter this morning ? "

" Yes," replied the men.

" Well," continued he, " your letter is not fair—it is not true ; and I think that before writing to me you have not reflected carefully upon all that you have written. Do you know what is in this letter ? "

" No," replied the workmen.

" How is this ? " said the employer. " Have you already forgotten what you wrote to me the day before yesterday ? "

" Oh, it was not we that wrote it," replied one of the foremen. " Stop, this was the way of it. A gentleman, well dressed, wearing a hat, alighted from a carriage a few days ago at the moment of our leaving the factory, and presented himself to us. ' Are you satisfied with your employer, gentlemen ?' he asked us. ' Thank God,' we replied, ' things are pretty well so far as concerns that matter.' ' So,' said he, with a contemptuous air, ' you would not desire that your miserable wages should be increased, nor your long hours of labour shortened ?' ' Yes, parbleu ! we should wish that.' ' All right,' said the gentleman in the hat; ' come then this evening to the Grande Place, to the rooms of the International; we will examine into your grievances against your employer, and before you strike we will send him a well-written letter, which will have its effect, I'll answer for it.' In the evening we went to ' La

Louve,' and while we were drinking a cup or so, there were two or three gentlemen writing at a desk. Afterwards, just as we were about to leave, they cried ' Silence ! silence !' and a gentleman who had got upon a table read something which nobody heard. I heard it said that it was a letter addressed to you in order that you might ameliorate the position of the working man."

" So then," interrupted the employer, " no one knows what was written ? " This remark produced death-like silence and a general shrugging of shoulders.

" Nevertheless," continued the employer triumphantly, " you have nearly all signed this letter. I have here in my hand eighty of your signatures ! "

" How ! how ! Our signatures ! " cried the men indignantly, " not a single man among us signed the letter."

" See," said the employer, " here are all your names."

" Our names as you will," was the reply ; " but by all the saints in paradise it was not we that wrote them ; we are ready to swear this."

" Listen," said the employer ; " I see that the person who wrote the letter has written also a great number of signatures ; but beside them are little crosses, such as are always made by those who do not write."

The workmen cried in chorus, " We have written

nothing. We have not even made a single cross. We have not held a pen in our hands. We will swear it."

After a little time the employer read the letter to the men, who admitted that it was both unjust and false, and they promised not to be so taken-in in future. The employer thought the autographs too curious to remain in private hands, and gave them into the charge of the Procureur du Roi.

429. *Budget of the International.*—One portion of the organization of the International, and that the most important—for the chiefs of course!—its budget, remains to be noticed. It is scarcely necessary to say that there is a total absence of official accounts; but the following details, referring to France and Belgium, will give some idea as to the way in which funds are raised and applied. Every member on his admission pays a fee of 50 centimes, for which he receives his admission card, which is renewed annually and gratuitously. He has also to pay a minimum annual tax of 10 centimes, to go towards the general expenses of the association. Then each federation imposes a special tax for its own expenses. At Lyons and Paris this amounts to 10 centimes per month. Thus it appears that the annual tax is very light, amounting only to 1 franc 30 cents, which is not paying too dear for the honour of belonging to a society that aspires to the government of the world, and commences by

burning it. But this honour may be had at a still cheaper rate; for the Swiss branch charges its members only 10 centimes a year. Yet even these small sums seem difficult to be got in, and the statutes are very severe upon defaulters. But there are taxes to pay to the sections, which raise the yearly contributions to 7 or 8 francs. Nor is this all. In the various legal prosecutions the society has had to undergo there is frequent reference to the *caisse fédérative du sou,* though the expression is nowhere exactly defined. So far as has been ascertained it alludes to a voluntary weekly subscription of 5 centimes, collected in workshops and factories, from workmen who did not belong to the association, but intended to join it, or to support it without joining it. In the statutes of the Parisian branch, art. 9 further says that the council may, if necessary, vote larger sums than the general budget would justify, and proportionately increase the amount of contributions payable by the members. But the most powerful arm of the association, when any particular object is to be attained, such for instance as the success of a strike, is subscription. Thus the successful termination of the strike in the building trade of Geneva in 1868, was thought of such importance as to call forth unusual exertions. But the delegate who was sent to London to collect subscriptions from the English workmen met with but slight success; not because these were niggardly, but because, in spite of their avowed hatred of state forms and aristocratic deliberation, they yet so closely imitate both, that the Genevese workmen might have been starved into submission before the English workmen had resolved to succour them, had not the Parisian workmen at once subscribed ten thousand francs. What these annual subscriptions may amount to, it is impossible to tell. No doubt the total is very great, considering the large number of members; and yet it is insufficient, in consequence of the strikes that are constantly taking place at all places and times. The journals are full of the fine phrases used by the chiefs of the International concerning the sufferings of the workmen reduced by infamous capitalists to the point of forsaking their work and of leaving the workshops where their misery is turned to account. A confidential letter of Varlin, one of the chiefs of the Paris federation, which was brought into court at the trial of the International on June 22, 1870, at Paris, however, shows that the chiefs do not speak quite so feelingly of these sufferings, when they are not expected to be heard by their dupes :—"This strike which we declared closed ten days ago, leaves four hundred workmen on our hands. The day before yesterday they wanted to destroy their former workshops and drive away the *mogs* that had taken their places. Fortunately we restrained them, but we are greatly bothered by this affair (*nous sommes bien embêtés par cette affaire*)." Poor misled work-men, leave, at the first order of your leaders, the shop where by honest labour you earn bread for yourselves and families! When the subscriptions which your fellow-workmen have raised are ex-hausted, pray do not trouble the chiefs who com-manded you to leave your work, for you might *bother* (*embêter*) them!

430. *The International and the Empire.*—At the time when the International was founded, the French Empire was as yet in all its strength. None of the parties that secretly strove against it seemed to have any chance of success; nor from their political and social characteristics could these parties, though all bent on the overthrow of the empire, coalesce and act as one combined force. The International refused to ally itself to any of them or to meddle with politics, but declared social questions paramount to all political considerations; and to the position thus assumed by the association it was due that the Imperial government did not molest it, but that the ministers allowed it to develop itself, hoping at the convenient moment to win it over to their interests. These ministers considered themselves very pro-found politicians, when they had fomented a quarrel between Prussia and Austria; trusting, when these two powers should mutually have exhausted each other, to seize the Rhenish provinces. They looked upon themselves as small Machiavellis when they

permitted the International to grow in order some day to use it against a mutinous bourgeoisie. The Emperor had an opportunity on September 2, at Sedan, and the Empress on September 4, at Paris, to judge of the value of such policy. However, the scheme of the association having been settled in London in 1864, the organizers opened at Paris a *bureau de correspondance,* which was neither formally interdicted nor regularly authorized by the Prefect and the Minister. But the constantly growing power of the International shown by the strikes of Roubaix, Amiens, Paris, Geneva, etc., after a time compelled the government either to direct or to destroy it. The Parisian manifesto read at Geneva was stopped at the French frontier; but M. Rouher agreed to admit it into France, if the association would insert some passages thanking the Emperor for what he had done for the working classes—a suggestion which was received with derision by the members. In the meantime the old revolutionary party, of which Mazzini, Garibaldi, Blanqui, and Ledru-Rollin were the oracles, looked with suspicion on the foundation of the International; for, as this last declared that it would not meddle with politics, the others called out, Treason! and thus the two parties were soon in a condition of violent opposition. In 1867, the Congress of Lausanne voted against war, but at the same moment the other fraction of the demagogues, assembled at Geneva, under pretence of forming a congress of *peace*, declared war to all tyrants and oppressors of the people. However, the two parties, the bourgeois demagogues and the workmen demagogues, eventually united; and thus it came to pass that by virtue of this pact the International took part in two revolutionary manifestations which occurred about six weeks after—the one at the tomb of Manin in the cemetery of Montmartre, and the other on the following day on the Boulevard Montmartre, to protest against the French occupation of Rome. The International having thus been carried away to declare war against the government, the latter determined to prosecute it. The association was declared to be dissolved, and fifteen of the leaders were each fined 100 francs. The International taking no notice of the decree of dissolution, a second prosecution was instituted, and nine of the accused were condemned to imprisonment for three months. The International now hid itself amidst the multitude of working men's societies of all descriptions that were either authorized or at least tolerated, and made enormous progress, so that its chiefs at last declared themselves able to do without any extraneous support. The International, said one of the speakers at the Bâle Congress (1869), is and must be a state within states; let these go on as suits them, until our state is the strongest. Then, on the ruins of these, we shall erect our own fully prepared, such as it exists in every section. The *Volksstimme*, the Austrian organ of the society, says: —"To us the red flag is the symbol of universal love of mankind. Let our enemies beware, lest they transform it against themselves into a flag of terror." To have an organ of its own the International founded the *Marseillaise*, with Rochefort for its chief, his association therewith having induced certain capitalists to find the necessary funds. Another personage with whom it became connected, and who afterwards became infamous, was the *soi-disant* General Cluseret, who had been expelled from the French army for dishonourable acts. He afterwards held a military command in the Fenian society, and devised in 1866, as a part of an Irish insurrection, the diversion of burning Downing Street and the principal public buildings of London. But the government were forewarned; and some of the members of the Irish Committee objected to the scheme. Cluseret, as an adventurer, always on the look-out for what might turn up, saw the power such an association as the International might command, and the latter found in him a willing tool. From a letter he addressed from New York to Varlin, on February 17, 1870, it also appears that all the crimes of which he has since then been guilty, were premeditated, and that he had from the first resolved not to perish without involving Paris in his fall. " On that day " (of the downfall of Louis Napoleon), he says, " on that day, we or nothing. On that day Paris must be ours or Paris must cease to exist." That this feeling was shared by other members of the association may be inferred from the fact that, at the house of one of the affiliated was found a dictionary which formed the key of their secret correspondence. Now, besides the usual words, we find such as nitroglycerine and picrate of potash; if the word petroleum does not occur in it, it is because the Prussians had not yet then taught these noble citizens the readiest means of burning down towns. At the house of another, recipes were discovered for the manufacture of nitro-glycerine, and of various other explosive compounds. Some of the recipes were followed by such directions as these :—" To be thrown in at windows," " to be thrown into gutters," etc. The attempted plebiscite in support of the reforms voted by the Senate, in January, 1870, was violently opposed by the International, who declared in favour of a republic. On the occasion of the plot of the Orsini shells, the society, in defending itself against the charge of having had any share in it, declared that it did not war against individual perpetrators of *coups d'état*, but that it was a permanent conspiracy of all the oppressed, which shall exist until all capitalists, priests, and political adventurers shall have disappeared. Such a declaration of war against all men that had any interest in the maintenance of public order, and especially against many men forming the then Imperial government, naturally induced a third prosecution.

Thirty-eight members were indicted, many of whom we meet again as active members of the Commune. Some were acquitted, others condemned to one year's imprisonment. No one suspected that the names of these obscure workmen, condemned as members of a secret society, would soon be connected with the most horrible disasters of Paris; and that these men, sentenced to such slight punishments, would at the end of a year re-appear before a military tribunal, after having for two months and a half filled terrified Paris with pillage, murder, and incendiary fires.

431. *The International and the War.*—The International condemns all war except war against bourgeois, capitalists, monopolists, parasites—that is to say, the classes that live not by manual labour, but by intellectual work, or the savings of any kind of labour. It abolishes national wars, to replace them by social war. For this reason it so pertinaciously insists on the abolition of all standing armies, which are of course great obstacles to its own plans. It therefore protested against the Franco-Prussian war, but as this opposition ended in mere talk, it need not further be dilated on. Its only results were to consign some of the most violent opponents to prison; and there is no proof

that one single soldier of the regular Prussian army, or even of the *Landwehr,* deserted or refused to fight, in order to remain faithful to the theories of the society. In France the affiliated of the International were only brave in civil war.

432. *The International and the Revolution.*—It is impossible in this section to be as precise and complete as could be desired; the events referred to are too recent, and the documents to be depended on are as yet in the hands of military tribunals and state prosecutors. The following, however, will be found to give a general outline of the events after the fall of the Napoleonic dynasty.

The demagogues were most noisy in demanding arms to defend the country, but they had no intention of turning them against the foreigner. Their sinister projects were sufficiently indicated by the murder of the *pompiers* of La Villette. Let it not be forgotten that on that day, close to the place where the crime was committed, a meeting of the International was to have taken place, which was forbidden at the last moment, and that its members were thronging the street at the very time the post of the *pompiers* was attacked. Let it also be borne in mind that one of the assassins, Eudes, condemned to death for his participation in the crime, and set free a few days after, became, after March 18, one of the generals of the Commune.

On September 3, the disaster of Sedan became

known at Paris. On the next day Lyons, Marseilles, Toulouse, and Paris proclaimed the Republic. This simultaneous movement was the result of an understanding existing between the leading members of the International in the various parts of France; but that the "Jules Favres and Gambettas," that *vermine bourgeoise,* as the International called them, should obtain any share of power, was very galling to the demagogues. At Lyons and Marseilles, however, the supreme power fell into the hands of the lowest wretches. The Commune installed at Lyons began its work by raising the red flag—that of the International. At Paris the association pretended at first to be most anxious to fight the Prussians. When the battalions were sent to the front, however, it was found that those comprising most Internationals were the most ready "to fall back in good order," or even to fly in great disorder at the first alarm; and General Clement Thomas pointed out this instructive fact to the readers of the *Journal Officiel.* But when a few Prussian regiments entered Paris, the International, through its central committee, announced that the moment for action was come; and so the members seized the cannons scattered in various parts of the city, and then began that series of excesses, for which the Commune will always enjoy an infamous notoriety. Its first sanguinary act was the assassination of Generals Lecomte and Clement Thomas. Some additional details on the Communists will be found in succeeding paragraphs.

433. *The International and the Commune.*—One would have supposed that the International would disavow the Communists; but, on the contrary, it approved of their proceedings. Flames were still ascending from the Hôtel de Ville, when already numerous sections of the International throughout Europe expressed their admiration of the conduct of the Parisian outcasts.

At Zurich, at a meeting of the members of the International, it was declared that " the struggle maintained by the Commune of Paris was just and worthy, and that all thinking men ought to join in the contest."

At Brussels the Belgian section of the International protested against the prosecution of the malefactors of Paris. At Geneva, two days before the entrance of the Versaillais into Paris, an address to the Commune was voted, declaring that it (the Commune) represented " the economic aspirations of the working classes." The German Internationalists were no less positive in their praise of the Communists:—" We are ready to defend the acts of the Commune at all times, and against all comers," says a socialistic paper published at Leipsic. The Italians sent an address to the Commune, ending thus:—" To capital which said, Ye shall starve, they replied : We will live by our labour. To des-

potism they replied : We are free ! To the cannons and chassepots of the réactionnaires they opposed their naked breasts. They fell, but fell as
heroes ! Now the reaction calls them bandits.
Shall we permit it ? No ! Let us invite our
brethren to our homes, and protect them. The
principles of the Commune are ours ; we accept the
responsibility of their acts." The English Internationalists were too few to prove their approbation of
the Commune by any public demonstration ; but
in private they did so very energetically. One of
the members even declared that the good time
" was really coming." " Soon," said he, " we
shall be able to dethrone the Queen of England,
turn Buckingham Palace into a workshop, and pull
down the York column, as the noble French people
has pulled down the Vendôme column." (Be it
observed here, that as this column chiefly comme-
morated French victories over the Germans, this
act of vandalism has by some authorities been attributed to the influence of Prussian gold liberally
distributed to certain patriotic members of the
Commune.) But the London section of the International has clearly put forth its views on the conduct of the Commune. The pamphlet, " The Civil
War in France," published for the council by Truelove, 256, High Holborn, the office of the International, is a continuous panegyric on the Commune,
and was at first signed by all the members of the

council; but two of them, Lucraft and Odger, have since then had their names withdrawn, stating that they had, in the first instance, been appended without their knowledge—which appeared to be the fact. Ought government to allow a society, proclaiming such principles, to exist and extend its pernicious influence?

434. *Parisian Communists.*—A few days before the entrance of the Versailles troops into Paris, about 200 men and 100 women were assembled, drinking and smoking, in a large room in the Rue Ménilmontant, at Paris. The men wore the uniform of the national guard; the women either common female apparel, or uniforms of a nondescript kind. All these persons, whose repulsive and vicious physiognomies were visible by the pale light of a dozen petroleum lamps, when not engaged with their glasses or pipes, were either singing patriotic songs or indulging in noisy conversation. It was about half-past eight, when a man wearing a captain's uniform entered the room. All faces at once turned towards him, and he was received with an universal shout of satisfaction. The new-comer was about twenty-eight years of age, tall and well made, and in his whole personal appearance and manner superior to the rabble around him.

"At last!" exclaimed a woman; "here is the president; we scarcely expected him any more to-night."

"Citizens!" cried the captain, "I beg your pardon for having kept you waiting; but I was delayed by an order from the Commune." Having ascended a kind of platform on which there was an arm-chair, he continued:—"Citizens, I have a secret communication to make to you. Are you quite certain that no stranger has got in amongst you?"

"Yes, yes!" cried several voices; "you may speak without fear."

The orator continued:—"It is well. My brave comrades, I trust your opinions have undergone no change; you are always true republicans, ready to sacrifice your existence for the Commune!" A somewhat ominous silence followed this appeal, which was succeeded by an almost universal expression of want of confidence in the leaders of the Commune, to which the captain replied by extolling the men now at the head of affairs.

"This is all very well," exclaimed a sergeant, "but the fact is, in spite of the bulletins of victory with which the walls of Paris are placarded every day, we are daily losing ground."

"That's true! that's true!" howled the rest.

"The fort of Issy is no longer ours . . . this loss has been a great blow to us."

"Well, my children," continued the captain, "I am to some extent of your opinion . . . and I have another piece of bad news to announce . . . we have lost the fort of Vanves."

These words were followed by cries of rage, threats, and horrible oaths.

" Then let us surrender," cried a young woman; " all is lost."

" Yes! No!"

" All this is dreadful, I know," said the captain; " but men like us must not give in. Do you want to know my opinion?"

"Yes, yes!"

" Well, before a week is over, the royalists will have made several other breaches in our walls; they will enter Paris by three different gates. This is only what we could have expected all along. But do you think that this will insure the victory of the Versaillais? By no means. Have we not terrible barricades, behind which we shall place the cannons and mitrailleuses to sweep down the enemy? Is not every house a fortress? We fire from windows, roofs, and coping-stones. It will be a hand-to-hand fight; and you will see that the troops will fraternize with us."

" But what about the Prussians?" observed a young man.

"What! do you think that when they see us win, they will fight us? No; they will find it to their interest to side with the victorious party, whichever it may be."

" That's true, that's true!"

The same sergeant, who had once before interrupted the speaker, now arose again, saying:—

" Citizens, I agree with our chief. The street-war can only benefit us. However, we must be prepared for everything; should we be beaten, what is to be done? Shall we surrender, like the traitors of Sedan? Never! If we become the victims of the drama about to be played, we demand a terrible vengeance; and if, unable to defend Paris, we surrender it, let us surrender it in ashes! Yes, let them not have the benefit of the beauty of Paris; let us burn down the monuments and houses, let us bury our enemies under its ruins. Our blood will flow, it is true, but let the Seine be red with theirs. If we must give up this city, let the conqueror die by the side of the conquered, in the same flames and under the same ruins!"

" Yes," continued the captain, " the Commune has provided for all; everything is prepared as if for a fairy spectacle. In all the monuments we have placed barrels of powder and petroleum; men will be stationed ready to set fire to them at the first signal. . . . Citizens, in the name of the Commune, I declare to you, that if we die we shall have a splendid funeral, and that Paris shall die with us."

" Bravo!" cried the maddened assembly. " Yes, death and fire everywhere. This shall be our vengeance—a true republican vengeance."

And the glasses were re-filled and fresh pipes were lighted.

435. *Character and Doings of the Commune.*—

The Versaillais have entered Paris, but different portions of the city are still held by the Communists. A party of them enter the house of the restaurateur Ronceray:—"Give up your house," says a captain; "we shall here hide our men to fire on the troops."

"Take what you like," was the reply of the proprietor, who with his waiters was about to make his escape. The Communists stopped them. "What more do you want?" he exclaimed. "You have my house, keep it, but let me and my people go."

"No, you must join us."

"What! *I* fire on Frenchmen?—never!"

They wanted to force arms upon him and the waiters; all refused to receive them.

"Shoot the traitors!" cried the captain.

Fifteen shots told upon the restaurateur and his waiters, whose bodies were thrown out of the windows and remained all day on the pavement.

*　　　*　　　*　　　*

Another set entered the Theatre of the Porte-Saint-Martin with a pail full of petroleum and a brush. These men went on the stage and coated the walls and scenery with that horrible oil, and then set fire to it; in less than two hours the theatre was burnt down.

A third set knocked at the door of the Theatre of the Délassements-Comiques, which was closed. M. Goetchy, the manager, was sent for. "Open!" cried the Communists. At first he refused, but had to yield in the end. Some of the men rushed into the building, carrying with them two bottles of petroleum; the keeper of the refreshment bar had to furnish matches, and the theatre was quickly set on fire. M. Goetchy's partner, M. de Jallais, and his wife, had concealed themselves in the cellars; fortunately for them the passers-by in the street succeeded in rescuing them. This theatre had been condemned beforehand by Raoul Rigault, who, as the lover of a woman who acted on that stage, had examined the building with a view to its wanton destruction.

*   *   *   *

When the Communists saw the necessity of giving up some particular position, they detached from their ranks a hundred men who, by fives, went into the houses to be destroyed, and addressed the concierges, saying:—" In ten minutes we shall set your house on fire; let your lodgers know, that they may escape." Any appeal was vain; their invariable answer was:—" The Commune wills it." And in the midst of cannon balls and bullets flying about in all directions, old men, women, and children, uttering cries of horror, endeavoured to make their escape. As to the young men found concealed, they were dragged to the barricade, and if they refused to fire on their fellow-countrymen they were shot without mercy. Thanks to petroleum, the houses burnt quickly. Many families that had sought refuge from shells in the cellars of their houses were buried under the ruins. Piles of corpses were found in many a cellar.

436. *Raoul Rigault.*—This worthless fellow during the empire meddled with conspiracy, and lived on the money he received from the republican committee. He lived at Belleville, was the constant companion of unfortunates, and spent his evenings at cabarets and casinos. That such a ruffian was elected a member of the Commune by more than two thousand votes sufficiently shows the character of the whole body. Like all the wretches who formed an integral portion of that criminal Commune, Rigault had no political convictions; he was a republican from interest. During the two months that he was in power, he squandered money most lavishly; and as a proof that he stole a great deal, Marie Dupuis, his mistress, always had her hands full of banknotes. He and his secretary, Dacosta, were in the habit of spending about seventy francs on their daily breakfasts. A search made at the lodgings of his mistress led to the discovery of a curious document, the will of Rigault, in which he makes her universal legatee. The Commune was profitable to Rigault; a few months before, he existed on loans exacted from or swindled out of his acquaintances. It was he who caused the hostages imprisoned in La Roquette to be shot. He was himself executed next day in the garden of the Luxembourg.

437. *Courbet.*—This person was, as a painter, possessed of some talent, but, as a man, was altogether worthless ; jealous of his confrères, he would fain have crushed them all. His artistic reputation did not satisfy him. Like Rochefort, he dreamt of red laurels, even should he be compelled to gather them in the blood of his friends—of people who in his evil days had stretched out a helping hand to him. He was arrested in his own house, where he had concealed himself in a cupboard. It is alleged that on being caught he exclaimed :—" Well, all right! I was nearly stifled."

438. *Assassination of Generals Lecomte and Clement Thomas.*—This double murder was the début of the International's interference in the war. It occurred on March 18, the first day of the revolution. Lecomte met the insurgents almost as a friend; he had given his men no orders to fire. Clement Thomas, in civilian's clothes, was wandering about in the neighbourhood of Belleville, looking out for some *chefs de bataillon* he wished to consult. A company of the national guard arrested these two generals, tied their hands behind their backs, and led them into an isolated garden ; there a captain, drunk with brandy, interrogated them, but they did not condescend to answer him. Immediately a council of war, composed of the said captain, a lieutenant, and some privates, was constituted ; and the generals were condemned to be shot. They were

immediately dragged before a wall, and ten men were invited to become their executioners. There was a perfect dispute among the soldiers as to who should perform the criminal task, they were all so eager for it. At last the ten men took their places. "Have you anything to say before you die?" asked a lieutenant. "Yes," replied General Thomas, "I have to tell you that you are cowards and assassins!" " Fire ! " commanded the captain. The generals fell. Thomas died at once, Lecomte breathed a few minutes longer. Some of the privates took up the corpses, and carried them through some of the streets of Montmartre, exclaiming, " Let the people's justice pass ! " A band of women and children followed the *cortége*, singing the *Marseillaise*. The bodies were left all night in a small house ; but, of course, the watches, rings, and purses of the two generals had before then found their way into the pockets of some honest Communists, both male and female.

439. *The Pétroleuses.*—These wretches were not so numerous as has been asserted. Their number amounted to about two hundred, and they had been discharged from Saint-Lazare by the Commune, on condition of setting Paris on fire. On the entrance of the Versaillais a great number of them were shot down at once.

A wounded officer had fallen down in the Rue d'Angoulême, and asked for a drink of water. One of these women heard him, and going up to him as if to succour him, stuck her dagger into his heart. Fortunately she was at once arrested and shot on the spot.

A fire had broken out near the Bastille, but the inhabitants made efforts to extinguish it by forming a chain of buckets. They had nearly succeeded, when suddenly three women crept in among the workers, and threw on a still burning spot three bucketfuls of petroleum. The flames broke forth again, but the three women were seized and thrown into their midst, where they were quickly consumed.

440. *The International's Comment.*—Of this Commune, the International, in its pamphlet, " The Civil War in France," says :—" The self-sacrificing heroism with which the population of Paris, men, women, and children, fought for eight days after the entrance of the Versaillais, reflects as much the grandeur of their cause, as the infernal deeds of the soldiery reflect the innate spirit of that civilization of which they are the mercenary vindicators." And again :—" In their stead, the real women of Paris showed again at the surface, heroic, noble, and devoted, like the women of antiquity. Working, thinking, fighting, bleeding Paris—almost forgetful, in its incubation of a new society, of the cannibal at its gates—radiant in the enthusiasm of its historic initiative !—working men's Paris, with

its Commune, will be for ever celebrated as the glorious harbinger of a new society. Its martyrs are enshrined in the great heart of the working classes!" And this of people of whom one of their own countrymen says :—"The Communists fight very bravely, it is true, but they get drunk to be courageous, which renders their wounds mortal. . . . The Commune has its police, yea, even its *mouchards*. . . . All these members of the Commune have their pockets full of gold, yet among them I recognize many that a year ago were needy vagabonds, living by borrowing, and wearing worn-out shoes. But none of these parasites, these rogues, were afraid to apply to the Commune and to ask for the best appointments. And the Commune had no choice. Besides, it well understood that to have faithful servants, it needed people without a spark of honour, that would not recoil from theft or any other infamy." The majority, in fact, of the members of the Commune were the scum of society. The International reproaches Thiers with having suppressed the republican journals, but does not mention that the Commune prohibited the publication of *Le Bien Public*, *L'Opinion Nationale*, *La Cloche*, *Le Soir*, *La Liberté*, *Le Gaulois*, and *Figaro*, and when some of them continued to appear in spite of the prohibition, sent ruffians to snatch the papers out of the hands of persons reading them. Again, the International says :—"The Commune admitted all foreigners to the honour of dying for an immortal cause. ; . . . The Commune honoured the heroic sons of Poland by placing them at the head of the defenders of Paris." Here Dombrowski is evidently alluded to; but the International does not at the same time mention that this Dombrowski was accused of having forged Russian banknotes, and that before accepting the command offered to him by the Commune, he stipulated for the immediate payment to him of 100,000 francs, which were forwarded to him without delay. How little the great body of English working men sympathise with the International is shown by the fact that they made large preparations for a demonstration with regard to the expected arrival of Jules Favre in London; though this same Jules Favre was denounced by the International as a scoundrel living in concubinage with the wife of a drunkard resident in Algiers, and as having by a most daring concoction of forgeries, spread over many years, contrived to grasp, in the name of the children of his adultery, a large succession, which made him a rich man—all which was proved by a series of authentic legal documents, published by M. Millière, who was shot by order of Jules Favre !

441. *Vitality of the Socialist Fallacy.*—Every one who has had occasion to look through the specifications of mechanical inventions at any patent office, must have been struck with the constant recurrence of

the same exploded fallacies for producing perpetual motion. Each fresh patentee puts forth his scheme, the counterpart of which has been put forth a hundred times before him, and proved to be impracticable, as if it were something entirely original; he seems to be totally unconscious that the same plan has been tried over and over again, and has failed in every instance. So with social reformers. Communism is only cabbage warmed up, and therefore not very savoury. To go no further back than Comte, Saint-Simon, and Enfantin, we find that organized combinations of workmen, trades unions, co-operative societies, the abolition of laws favouring the accumulation of property, of standing armies and war, were to be the means of regenerating mankind. The converts then gained for these doctrines included civil engineers, barristers, officers in the army, men of position and fortune. The movement was regarded by Lacordaire as the most important since that of Luther. Yet it died out, because it is opposed to the influence of human passions, which after all rule the world. It died out, although some of the men that advocated these principles were perfectly honest in their aims, as Saint-Simon, for instance, of whom Béranger wrote—

J'ai vu Saint-Simon, le prophète,
Riche d'abord, puis endetté,
Qui des fondements jusqu'au faîte
Refaisait la société.

Plein de son œuvre commencée,
   Vieux, pour elle il tendait la main,
Sûr qu'il embrassait la pensée
   Qui doit sauver le genre humain.

Look at the subject of war. What can be more senseless and barbarous than fighting ? We ridicule duellists, and yet what are two nations going to war but duellists multiplied ? A government declares war against another, and immediately both countries are thrown into a ferment and fever of sanguinary excitement, though but very few of the natives of either state know anything of the justice or injustice of the quarrel. But most are ready to be led to slaughter, or to pay in purse for the mad trial of strength. And the working classes, who through their socialistic agitators express the greatest horror of war, are the most enthusiastic for it ; but this is easily explained—animal instincts predominate in them. The poet wrote long ago :—

" The time is past when sword subdued :
But the heart and the mind,
And the voice of mankind,
Shall arise in communion ;
And who shall resist that proud union ? "

And at the time of the first London Exhibition in 1851, a Quaker proposed that no weapons or engines of war should be displayed in the world's show, as it was to be the beginning of the era of peace ; trusting that reason and universal goodwill would thenceforth

govern the mutual dealings of men ; and a great
deal more of such ignorant, though well-meant
twaddle. Yet only a very few years after came that
Russian war for which none cried out more madly
than the working classes. The fact is, no civilization will ever put an end to war. As Napoleon said
of the Russian, " Scratch, and you will find the
Tartar underneath ;" so it may, with greater truth,
be said of every man of every country, " Scratch,
and you will find the devil underneath." The human
heart will ever be the same, and necessarily so, since
the seven properties of nature (11) work in and
rule through it eternally. Wherever there is light
there is darkness also, and the more intense the light
the more dense the darkness ; wherefore it happens
that the most civilized nations have invented the most
murderous weapons of war. And as Communism
will not abolish war, so will it not alter one single
feature of social life. If all capitalists were anni-
hilated to-day, and their possessions distributed
among millions of paupers, we should in a few years
have capitalists and " wages-slaves" again; for very
few would have either the skill or the self-command
profitably to invest and apply their newly-acquired
wealth. The story is as old as the hills, and yet
pushing demagogues and selfish agitators constantly
find fresh dupes to believe in the coming millennium
of labour, and contribute their pence to the gilding
of their self-elected idol. But workmen that have

money in the savings-bank do not worship it, nor help to adorn it. Hence Communism will never be anything but a scare-crow, even if it co-operate with the Ultramontanes, as it is doing in Belgium, forming a double-bodied monster of Black and Red Jesuits.

VIII.

PERMANENT REVOLUTION.

442.

ARIOUS Revolutionary Societies in France.—France, like Italy, has always been a centre of secret societies. One revolution is scarcely ended, before secret associations begin to prepare for another. Immediately after the July revolution, the students of the *Quartier Latin* of Paris formed the " Society of Order and Progress," each student being provided with a rifle and fifty cartridges, as the most orderly method of furthering progress. Another association, called the " Society of Schools," advocated the abolition of the universities and the throwing open of all instruction to the public gratuitously. The " Constitutional Society," directed by a man who had powerfully supported the candidature of the Duke of Orleans, Cauchois-Lemaire, insisted on the suppression of monopolies, the more equal levy of taxes, electoral reform, and the abolition of the dignity of the peerage. The " Friends of the People " was another political society, one section of

which, called the " Rights of Man," adopted for its
text-book the " Declaration of the Rights of Man "
by Robespierre, and drew to itself many minor societies, too numerous, and in most cases too unim-
portant, to be mentioned. Their efforts ended in
the useless insurrection of Lyons, on the 13th and
14th April, 1834. The Communist societies of the
Travailleurs Egalitaires and *Communistes Révolu-
tionnaires* introduced some of their members into
the provisional government that preceded the accession of Louis Napoleon; and their influence even
to the present day is too notorious to need specifica-
tion here. The " Mountaineers," or " Reds of the
Mountain," was one of the societies that brought
about the events of 1848. They swore on a dagger,
"I swear by this steel, the symbol of honour, to
combat and destroy all political, religious, and social
tyrannies." And that they meant it is proved by
various documents which were discovered, wherein
different rulers are on paper condemned to death;
sometimes the same sentence is found recorded
against a traitor in their own ranks. In one instance a certain Benjamin Richer, age twenty-six,
killed his mother by stabbing her nine times, for
having been, as he declared in court, " treacherous
and a coward," in preventing him from going out
fighting with his brethren, the Reds of the Mountain. Louis Napoleon made severe laws against all
secret societies, and sent some of the most prominent members to Cayenne.

IX.

YOUNG ITALY.

443.

*R**EVOLUTIONARY** Societies in Italy.*—Joseph Mazzini, who forty years ago was a prisoner in Fort Savona for revolutionary speeches and writings, may be looked upon as the chief instigator of modern secret societies in Italy having revolutionary tendencies. The independence and unity of their country, with Rome for its capital, of course were the objects of Young Italy.

Here are some of the articles of the " Organization of Young Italy : "—1. The society is founded for the indispensable destruction of all the governments of the Peninsula, in order to form one single state with the republican government. 2. Fully aware of the horrible evils of absolute power, and the even worse results of constitutional monarchies, we must aim at establishing a republic, one and indivisible. 30. Those who refuse obedience to the orders of this secret society, or reveal its mysteries, die by the dagger without mercy. 31. The secret tribunal pronounces sentence and appoints one or two affiliated members for its execution. 32. Who so refuses to perform such duty assigned to him, dies on the spot. 33. If the victim escapes, he shall be pursued, until struck by the avenging hand, were he on the bosom of his mother or in the temple of Christ. 34. Every secret tribunal is competent not only to judge guilty adepts, but to put to death any one it finds it necessary to condemn.—(Sig.) Mazzini.

Committees were established in all parts of the Peninsula; the presses, not only of Italy, but also of Marseilles, London, and Switzerland were largely employed to disseminate the views of the conspirators; and the police, though they considered themselves well informed, were always at fault. Thus Livio Zambeccari, a leading member, went from Bologna to Naples, thence into Sicily, held interviews with the conspirators, called meetings, and returned to Bologna, whilst the police of Naples and Sicily knew nothing at all about it. General Antonini, under a feigned name, went to Sicily, passed himself off for a daguerreotypist, and lived in great intimacy with many of the officials without being suspected. A Piedmontese officer, who had fought in the Spanish and Portuguese revolutionary wars, arrived at Messina under a Spanish name, with letters of introduction from a Neapolitan general, which enabled him to visit and closely inspect the citadels, this being the object of his journey. Letters from Malta, addressed to the conspirators, were intercepted by the police, but recovered from them before they had read them, by the address and daring of the members of Young Italy. A thousand copies of a revolutionary programme, printed at Marseilles, were smuggled into Italy in a despatch addressed to the minister Delcaretto. A revolutionary correspondence was carried on by means of the official letters addressed to the minister Santangelo, at Palermo. A well-known Spanish general, who was one of the conspirators, whose departure and object had been publicly announced in the French papers, went from Marseilles to Naples, and the police were unable to catch him.

444. *Various Societies.* — Such men were the emissaries of the various secret societies formed throughout Italy. Thus at Padua a society existed whose members called themselves *Selvaggi*, " Savages," because the German democrat, Marr, had said, that man must return to the savage state to accomplish something great. The members of the *Unità Italiana*, discovered at Naples in 1850, recognized each other by a gentle rubbing of noses. They swore on a dagger with a triangular blade, with the inscription, "Fraternity—Death to Traitors

—Death to Tyrants," faithfully to observe all the laws of the society, on pain, in case of want of faith, to have their hearts pierced with the dagger. Those who executed the vengeance of the society called themselves the Committee of Execution. In 1849 the grand council of ·the sect established a " Committee of Stabbers," *comitato de' pugnalatori.* The heads of the society were particular as to whom they admitted into it; the statutes say, "no ex-Jesuits, thieves, coiners, and other infamous persons are to be initiated." The ex-Jesuits are placed in good company truly !

In 1849 a society was discovered at Ancona calling itself the " Company of Death," and many assassinations, many of them committed in broad daylight in the streets of the town, were traced to its members. The " Society of Slayers," *Ammazzatori,* at Leghorn; the "Infernal Society," at Sinigaglia; the " Company of Assassins," *Sicarii,* at Faenza; the " Terrorists " of Bologna, were associations of the same stamp. The " Barbers of Mazzini," at Rome, made it their business to " remove " priests who had rendered themselves particularly obnoxious. Another Bolognese society was that of the " Italian Conspiracy of the Sons of Death," whose object was the liberation of Italy from foreign sway.

A secret. society of assassins has recently been discovered, and many of its members brought to trial, at Ravenna. Its existence had long been surmised, but the executive did not dare to interfere; some private persons, indeed, tried to bring the assassins to justice, but wherever they succeeded a speedy vengeance was sure to follow. To one shopkeeper who had been particularly active a notice was sent that his life was forfeited, and the same night a placard was posted up upon the shutters of his shop, announcing that the establishment was to be sold, as the proprietor was going away. In many cases there were witnesses to the crimes, and yet they dared not interfere nor give evidence. One of the gang at last turned traitor; he gave the explanation of several " mysterious disappearances," and the names of the murderers. The gang had become too numerous, and amongst the number there were members whose fidelity was suspected. It was resolved to sacrifice them. They were watched, set upon and murdered by their fellow-accomplices. This society was known as the *Accoltellatori*, literally " knifers "—cut-throats. It originally consisted of twelve members only, who used to meet in the café Mazzavillani—a very appropriate name; *mazza* means a club or bludgeon, and *villano*, villanous—at Ravenna, where the fate of their victims was decided. The trial is still proceeding (Nov. 1874).

445. *Italian Insurrections.*—Gregory XVI. died on the 1st of June, 1846. Mazzini thought this

the favourable moment for general action, and the revolutions of Rome, Naples, Palermo, Florence, Milan, Parma, Modena and Venice followed in quick succession. They are matter of current history; the war, begun by Mazzini and brought to a successful issue chiefly through Garibaldi, ended in the establishment of the Kingdom of United Italy, and the overthrow—for ever, it is to be hoped—of the pope's temporal powers. The name of Garibaldi has as much of magic power in it in Italy, as that of Napoleon still has in France; and Mazzini now has his marble statue in the Palazzo del Municipio at Genoa.

446. *Assassination of Rossi.*—But as we are more concerned with the secret action of secret societies than with their open deeds, this brief notice of Young Italy may fitly be closed with a short account of the assassination of Count Rossi, planned and executed by the Mazzinists. Rossi was born at Carrara, and began his public career as member of the provisional government of Bologna, when Murat attempted the conquest of Italy. At his master's defeat, he fled into Switzerland, where the Diet entrusted him with the revision of the pact of 1815; in the changes he proposed, radicalism was carried to its utmost limits, and aimed at the overthrow of the Federal Government. With such antecedents, it was but natural that Rossi became a member of Young Italy; though Mazzini placed no

faith in him, for he knew that the ci-devant Carbonaro had no fixed political convictions. For this once violent demagogue, having in the July revolution of 1830 assisted Louis-Philippe to ascend the French throne, accepted from him the title of count and peer of France, and was sent as ambassador to Rome. Though he had once belonged to the secret societies of Italy, and by Gregory XVI. been designated as the political renegade, he eventually accepted office under Pius IX., who in 1848, a short time before his flight from Rome, had no one to appeal to, to form a new ministry, but this very adventurer, who did so by keeping three of the portfolios in his own hands, viz. those of Finances, Interior and Police, whilst the other ministers mutually detested each other; a fact from which Rossi expected to derive additional advantages. His political programme, which excluded all national participation or popular influence, filled Young Italy with rage. At a meeting of young Italy, held at the hôtel Feder at Turin the verdict went forth: Death to the false Carbonaro! By a pre-arranged scheme the lot to kill Rossi fell on Canino, a leading man of the association, not that it was expected that he would do the deed himself, but his position and wealth were assumed to give him the most ready means of commanding daggers. A Mazzinian society assembled twice a week at the Roman theatre, Capranica. At a meeting of one hundred and sixteen members, it was decided, at the suggestion of Mazzini, that forty should be chosen by lot to protect the assassin. Three others were elected by the same process, they were called *feratori;* one of them was to slay the minister.

The 15th of November, the day fixed upon for the opening of the Roman Chambers, was also that of Rossi's death. He received several warnings, but ridiculed them. Even in going to the Chancellerie, he was addressed by a priest, who whispered to him: " Do not go out, you will be assassinated." " They cannot terrify me," he replied, " the cause of the Pope is the cause of God," which is thought by some to have been a very noble answer, but which was simply ridiculous, because not true; and was, moreover, vile hypocrisy on the part of a man with his antecedents. When Rossi arrived at the Chancellerie, the conspirators were already awaiting him there. One of them, as the minister ascended the staircase, struck him on the side with the hilt of a dagger, and as Rossi turned round to look at his assailant, another assassin plunged his dagger into Rossi's throat. The minister soon after expired in the apartments of Cardinal Gozzoli, to which he had been carried. At that very instant one of the chiefs of Young Italy at Bologna, looking at his watch, said: " A great deed has just been accomplished; we no

longer need fear Rossi." The estimation in which
Rossi was held by the Chamber cannot have been
great, for the deputies received the news of his
death with considerable sang-froid; and at night a
torch-light procession paraded the streets of Rome,
carrying aloft the dagger which had done the deed,
whilst thousands of voices exclaimed: "Blessed be
the hand that struck Rossi! Blessed be the dagger
that struck him!" A pamphlet published at Rome
in 1850 contains a letter from Mazzini, in which
occur the words, "The assassination of Rossi was
necessary and just."

P.S.—Since writing the above I have met with
documents which induce me to suspend my judg-
ment as to who were the real authors of Rossi's
assassination. From what I have since learnt it
would seem that the clerical party, and not the Carbonari, planned and executed the deed. Persons
accused of being implicated in the murder were
kept in prison for more than two years without
being brought to trial, and then quietly got away.
Rossi, shortly before his death, had levied contributions to the extent of four million scudi on clerical
property, and was known to plan further schemes
to reduce the influence of the Church. But the
materials for writing the history of those times are
not yet accessible.

BOOK XVII.

MISCELLANEOUS SOCIETIES.

AUTHORITIES.

Les Jésuites. Par Michelet et Quinet. Paris.

Destruction des Jésuites en France. Par D'Alembert. Paris.

Les Jésuites. Par A. Andréi. Paris.

Secreta Monita Societatis Jesu.

Histoire Intime de la Russie. Par J. H. Schnitzler. Bruxelles, 1847.

I.

MISCELLANEOUS SOCIETIES.

447.

THE *A B C Friends.*—A society whose avowed scope was the education of children; its real object the liberty of man. They called themselves members of the A B C, letters which in French are pronounced *abaissé;* but the abased that were to be raised were the people. The members were few but select. They had two lodges in Paris during the Restoration. Victor Hugo has introduced the society in *Les Misérables,* part iii. book iv.

448. *Academy of the Ancients.*—It was founded at Warsaw by Colonel Toux de Salverte, in imitation of a similar society and with the same name, founded in Rome towards the beginning of the sixteenth century. The object of its secret meetings was the cultivation of the occult sciences.

449. *Almusseri.*—This is an association similar to that of "Belly Paaro" (456), found among the negroes of Senegambia, and other parts of the

African continent. The rites of initiation bear some resemblance to the Orphic and Cabiric rituals. In the heart of an extensive forest there rises a temple, access to which is forbidden to the profane. The receptions take place once a year. *The candidate feigns to die.* At the appointed hour the initiated surround the aspirant and chant funereal songs; whereupon he is carried to the temple, placed on a moderately hot plate of copper, and anointed with the oil of the palm—a tree which the Egyptians dedicated to the sun, as they ascribed to it three hundred and sixty-five properties. In this position he remains forty days—this number, too, constantly recurs in antiquity—his relations visiting him to renew the anointing; after which period he is greeted with joyful songs, and conducted home. He is supposed to have received a new soul, and enjoys great consideration and authority among his tribe.

450. *Anonymous Society.*—This society also, which existed for some time in Germany, with a Grand Master resident in Spain, occupied itself with alchymy.

451. *Anti-Masons.*—This was a society founded in Ireland, in County Down, in 1811, and composed of Roman Catholics, whose object was the expulsion of all Freemasons, of whatever creed they might be.

452. *Apocalypse, Knights of the.*—This secret society was formed in Italy in 1693, to defend the Church against the expected Antichrist. Augustine

Gabrino, the son of a merchant of Brescia, was its founder. On Palm-Sunday, when the choir in Saint Peter's was intoning the words, *Quis est iste Rex Gloriæ?* Gabrino, carrying a sword in his hand, rushed among the choristers, exclaiming, *Ego sum Rex Gloriæ.* He did the same in the church of San Salvatore, whereupon he was shut up in a mad-house. The society, however, continued to flourish, until a wood-carver, who had been initiated, denounced it to the Inquisition, which imprisoned the knights. Most of them, though only traders and operatives, always carried a sword, even when at work, and wore on the breast a star with seven rays and an appendage, symbolizing the sword seen by St. John in the Apocalypse. The society was accused of having political aims. It is a fact that the founder called himself Monarch of the Holy Trinity, which is not extraordinary in a madman; and wanted to introduce polygamy, for which he ought to be a favourite with the Mormons.

453. *Areoiti.*—This is a society of Tahitian origin, and has members throughout that archipelago. They have their own genealogy, hierarchy, and traditions. They call themselves the descendants of the god Oro-Tetifa, and are divided into seven degrees, distinguished by the degrees of tattooing allowed to them. The society forms an institution similar to that of the Egyptian priests; but laymen also may be admitted. The chiefs at once attain to the high-

est degrees, but the common people must obtain their initiation through many trials. Members enjoy great consideration and many privileges. They are considered as the depositaries of knowledge, and as mediators between god and man; and are feared as the ministers of the *taboo*, a kind of excommunication they can pronounce, like the ancient hierophants of Greece or the court of Rome. Though the ceremonies are disgusting and immoral there is a foundation of noble ideas concealed under them; so that we may assume the present rites to be corruptions of a formerly purer ceremonial. The meaning that underlies the dogmas of the initiation is the generative power of nature. The legend of the solar god also here plays an important part and regulates the festivals; and a funereal ceremony, reminding us of that of the mysteries of antiquity, is performed at the winter solstice. Throughout Polynesia, moreover, there exists a belief in a supreme deity, *Taaroa* or *Tangaroa*, of whom a cosmogonic hymn, known to the initiated, says:—"He was; he was called *Taaroa;* he called, but no one answered; he, the only *ens*, transformed himself into the universe; he is the light, the germ, the foundation; he, the incorruptible; he is great, who created the universe, the great universe."

454. *Avengers, or Vendicatori.*—A secret society formed, about 1186, in Sicily, to avenge public wrongs, on the principles of the Vehm (166) and Beati Paoli (173). At length Adiorolphus of Ponte Corvo,

Grand Master of the sect, was hanged by order of King William II. the Norman, and many of the sectaries were branded with a hot iron.

455. *Babismo.*—This religious sect, tinctured with political tendencies, exists among the Persians; and is connected with Freemasonry, introduced from France.

456. *Belly Paaro.* — Among the negroes of Guinea there are mysteries called " Belly Paaro," which are celebrated several times in the course of a century. The aspirant, having laid aside all clothing, and every precious metal, is led into a large wood, where the old men that preside at the initiation, give him a new name, whilst he recites verses in honour of the god, Belly, joins in lively dances, and receives much theological and mystical instruction. The neophyte passes five years in absolute isolation, and woe to any woman that dares to approach the sacred wood ! After this noviciate the aspirant has a cabin assigned to him, and is initiated into the most secret doctrines of the sect. Issuing thence, he dresses differently from the others, his body being adorned with feathers, and his neck showing the scars of the initiatory incisions.

457. *Camisards.* — Protestant peasants of the Cévennes, who rose up against Louis XIV. on his revocation of the Edict of Nantes, at the instigation of the Jesuits. They wore shirts over their clothes, hence the name. Between 1702 and 1704,

30,000 Cévenols are said to have perished in war, or in less lawful massacre, or on the scaffold. A greater number still of the king's troops were destroyed ; and some of the greatest captains in France earned only failure and disgrace when opposed to simple mountaineer leaders like Roland, or the shepherd boy, Cavalier.

458. *Charlottenburg, Order of.*—This was one of the numerous branches grafted on the trunk of the Union of Virtue.

459. *Church Masons.*—This is a Masonic rite, founded in this country during this century, with the scarcely credible object of re-establishing the ancient Masonic trade-unions.

460. *Camorra.*—This Italian society possessed, up to recent times, great political influence, now a rival of, now co-operating with the Carbonari, and Ciro Annichiarico (386) was more of a Camorrist than a Carbonaro. Under the late Bourbon government of Naples, the Camorra was at the zenith of its power, and when Francis II. in September, 1860, left his capital exposed to the horrors and dangers of a social conflagration, and whilst the magistrates, deprived of all authority and power, felt themselves unable to cope with the anarchy reigning around, the Camorrist chiefs had influence enough to avert the danger. They promised that public order should not be disturbed ; and from the moment of the king's departure to

the arrival of Garibaldi, not the least disturbance occurred. The society still exists in a degenerate state, being now composed of criminals only. On the 3rd September, 1873, the Neapolitan police surprised the committee of the Camorra, assembled at an *osteria* or inn in the Strada Floria, and sixteen individuals, all well armed, and almost all of them implicated in various crimes, were arrested. At Naples and in its neighbourhood every unexplained murder is now attributed to this society.

P.S.—Since the above was written, the Camorristi have been brought prominently before the world by the wholesale arrests of members of the gang recently made at Naples. As stated in the text, the society has lost all political aims or significance, consisting of criminals only, some of them, however, belonging to classes above the rabble. Its chief pursuit now is extortion. Trades-people, flymen, hotel-keepers, and other persons engaged in business are put under contribution to this society, "in the name of the people, and to maintain the rights and independence of the people." The fear the Camorra inspires is so great that it is difficult, nay, sometimes impossible, to obtain witnesses against any of its members. An occasional correspondent of the "Times" at Naples reports a case where a chief Camorristo named Del Giudice murdered a companion one night outside a theatre. There could be no doubt, for several witnesses were present. The murderer was arrested, and brought up for trial in August last; but on the day appointed the court was thronged with well-known Camorristi; the Procureur-Général had received a threatening letter, so had the jury and the witnesses. The latter gave their evidence in such a manner as to be of no value, and the assassin could not be convicted, the jury returning a verdict of *non constat,* "not proven." It is to be hoped that the Italian government will persevere in the vigorous course it has now initiated against the lawless associations still existing, such as Camorristi and brigands.

461. *Cougurde.*—One of the many forms assumed by the Liberal party in France, during the Bourbon restoration. From the town of Aix it spread through Provence.

462. *Dervishes.*—Also called Fakirs, and a monastic order of Islamism. Mahomet prohibited the introduction of monks into his religious system; but thirty years after the death of the Prophet, monks made their appearance, and it is supposed that there are now seventy-two orders of them. But twelve of them are undoubtedly older than Islamism. Some of them practise jugglers' tricks, such as swallowing daggers, eating fire, etc. The latter may remind us of the Etruscan priests of Phœbus. The most important of these orders is that of Mewlewi, on account of its poetic mysticism, and its doctrine that light is the first-born of

God. The Dervishes are England's great enemies in India, ever striving to inspire the Mahomedan population with a hatred of British rule; and the belief is widely spread that the Freemasons are in secret connection with them. The Freemasons in connection with the Dervishes ! Who ever heard that the Dervishes brew good beer? A short time ago, the Assistant Secretary to the Municipality of Lahore, Mr. Bull, was struck down by a fakir, a religious mendicant of one of the most dangerous fanatical sects in India. Whenever mischief is astir among the Mussulman populations, these men are at the bottom of it. The attack upon Mr. Bull was regarded at the time as indicative of a connection between the Hindoo Sikhs and the Mussulman population of the Punjaub.

463. *Etherists.*—This was a Greek society founded at the end of the last or the beginning of the present century, to render their country independent. The first idea of it is ascribed to the poet Riga, who was by Austria betrayed into the power of Turkey, where he was executed in a barbarous manner in 1798. Even during the Venetian rule many Greeks attended the Italian universities, and these students formed an Etheria to reconstruct the Greek empire. Led on by the promises of Napoleon, the Etherists prepared to make a descent on Greece from the Ionian Islands; but the fall of the emperor frustrated the scheme. It was revived at

Vienna in 1815, and the Count Capo d'Istria obtained a promise of assistance from the Emperor of Russia. The Etherists now called themselves " Friends of the Muses," and seemed to form a society for the investigation of the literary and archæological antiquities of Greece, though their aspirations were very different. Their chief seat was at Munich. The sect gradually grew more influential, and began to show its political tendencies. It introduced itself into the Morea, and prepared the Greeks for a great national event. They, however, in 1819, sent an agent to St. Petersburg to ascertain the disposition of that court in case of a Greek rising; but, obtaining nothing beyond vague promises, the Etherists elected for their chief Alexander Ypsilanti, and made the necessary preparations for the movement which took place in the following year.

464. *Fraticelli.*—A sect who were said to have practised the custom of self-restraint under the most trying circumstances of disciplinary carnal temptation. They were found chiefly in Lombardy; and Pope Clement V. preached a crusade against them, and had them extirpated by fire and sword, hunger and cold. But they were guilty of a much higher crime than the one for which they were ostensibly persecuted; they had denounced the tyranny of the popes, and the abuses of priestly power and wealth, which of course de-

served nothing less than extermination by fire and sword !

465. *Goats, The.*—About the year 1770 the terri- tory of Limburg was the theatre of strange proceed- ings. Churches were sacked, castles burnt down, and robberies were committed everywhere. The country-people were trying to shake off the yoke feudalism had imposed on them. During the night, and in the solitude of the *landes*, the most daring assembled and marched forth to perpetrate these devastations. Then terror spread everywhere, and the cry was heard, "The Goats are coming !" They were thus called because they wore masks in imita- tion of goats' faces over their own. On such nights the slave became the master, and abandoned himself with fierce delight to avenging the wrongs he had suffered during the day. In the morning all dis- appeared, returning to their daily labour, whilst the castles and mansions set on fire in the night were sending their lurid flames up to the sky. The greater the number of malcontents, the greater the number of Goats, who at last became so numerous that they would undertake simultaneous expeditions in different directions in one night. They were said to be in league with the devil, who, in the form of a goat, was believed to transport them from one place to another. The initiation into this sect was performed in the following manner:—In a small chapel situate in a dense wood, a lamp was lighted

during a dark and stormy night. The candidate
was introdued into the chapel by two godfathers,
and had to run round the interior of the building
three times on all-fours. After having plentifully
drunk of a strong fermented liquor, he was put
astride on a wooden goat hung on pivots. The
goat was then swung round, faster and faster, so
that the man, by the strong drink and the motion,
soon became giddy, and sometimes almost raving
mad; when at last he was taken down, he was easily
induced to believe that he had been riding through
space on the devil's crupper. From that moment
he was sold, body and soul, to the society of Goats,
which, for nearly twenty years, filled Limburg with
terror. In vain the authorities arrested a number
of suspected persons; in vain, in all the communes,
in all the villages, gibbet and cord were in constant
request. From 1772-74 alone the tribunal of
Foquemont had condemned four hundred Goats to
be hanged or quartered. The society was not ex-
terminated till about the year 1720. *₤ /₅₂c*

466. *Hare's Foot, Society of the.*—This was a
society formed in Canada against the English
Government.

467. *Huséanawer.*—The natives of Virginia gave
this name to the initiation they conferred on their
own priests, and to the noviciate those not belonging
to the priesthood had to pass through. The candidate's body was anointed with fat, and he was led

before the assembly of priests, who held in their hands green twigs. Sacred dances and funereal shouts alternated. Five youths led the aspirant through a double file of men armed with canes to the foot of a certain tree, covering his person with their bodies and receiving in his stead the blows aimed at him. In the meantime the mother prepared a funeral pyre for the simulated sacrifice, and wept her son as dead. Then the tree was cut down, and its boughs lopped off and formed into a crown for the brows of the candidate, who during a protracted retirement, and by means of a powerful narcotic called *visocean*, was thrown into a state of somnambulism. Thence he issued among his tribe again and was looked upon as a new man, possessing higher powers and higher knowledge than the non-initiated.

468. *Invisibles, The.*—We know not how much or how little of truth there is in the accounts, very meagre indeed, of this society, supposed to have existed in Italy in the last century, and to have advocated, in nocturnal assemblies, atheism and suicide.

469. *Jesuits.*—The Jesuits can scarcely be called a secret society. Still their influence on secret societies has often been great, and in all parts of the world they have always had a vast number of affiliates, who, though not openly belonging to the order, were bound to propagate its principles and

protect its interests—such men as in France are called *Jésuites de robe courte.* There is considerable analogy and similitude between Masonic and Jesuitic degrees; the Jesuits tread down the shoe and bare the knee, because Ignatius Loyola thus presented himself at Rome and asked for the confirmation of the order. The initials of the Masonic pass-words correspond exactly with those of the Jesuit officers: *Temporalis* (Tubalcain); *Scholasticus* (Shibboleth); *Coadjutor* (Ch (g) iblum); *Noster* (Notuma). Many other analogies might be established. Not satisfied with confession, preaching, and instruction, whereby they had acquired unexampled influence, they formed in Italy and France, in 1563, several " Congregations," *i. e.,* clandestine meetings held in subterranean chapels and other secret places. The congregationists had a sectarian organization, with appropriate catechisms and manuals, which had to be given up before death, wherefore very few copies remain. In the library of the Rue Richelieu at Paris there is a MS. entitled, *Histoire des congrégations et sodalités jésuitiques depuis* 1563 *jusqu'au temps présent* (1709).

470. *Initiations.*—From this, as well as other works, we gather some of the ceremonies with which aspirants were initiated into the Order. Having in nearly all Roman Catholic countries succeeded in becoming the educators of the young, they were able to mould the youthful mind according to their

secret aims. If then, after a number of years, they detected in the pupil a blind and fanatic faith, conjoined with exalted pietism and indomitable courage, they proceeded to initiate him; in the opposite case, they excluded him. The proofs lasted twenty-four hours, for which the candidate was prepared by long and severe fasting, which, by prostrating his bodily strength, inflamed his fancy, and just before the trial a powerful drink was administered to him. Then the mystic scene began—diabolical apparitions, evocation of the dead, representations of the flames of hell, skeletons, moving skulls, artificial thunder and lightning, in fact, the whole paraphernalia and apparatus of the ancient mysteries. If the neophyte, who was closely watched, showed fear or terror, he remained for ever in the inferior degree; but if he bore the proof well, he was advanced to a higher grade. There were four degrees. The first consisted of the *Coadjutores Temporales,* who performed the manual labour and merely servile duties of the Order; the second embraced the *Scholastici,* from among whom the teachers of youth were chosen; the third was composed of the *Coadjutores Spirituales,* which title was given to the members when they took the three vows of the Society. The *Professi* formed the fourth and highest grade; they alone were initiated into all the secrets of the Order.

At the initiation into the second degree, the same proofs, but on a grander scale, had to be undergone.

The candidate, again prepared for them by long fastings, was led with his eyes bandaged into a large cavern, resounding with wild howlings and roarings, which he had to traverse, reciting at the same time prayers specially appointed for that occasion. At the end of the cave he had to crawl through a narrow opening, and while doing this, the bandage was taken from his eyes by an unseen hand, and he found himself in a square dungeon, whose floor was covered with a mortuary cloth, on which stood three lamps, shedding a feeble light on the skulls and skeletons ranged around. This was the Cave of Evocation, the Black Chamber, so famous in the annals of the Fathers. Here giving himself up to prayer, the neophyte passed some time, during which the priests could, without his being aware of it, watch his every movement and gesture. If his behaviour was satisfactory, all at once two brethren, representing archangels, presented themselves before him, without his being able to tell whence they had so suddenly started up,—a good deal can be done with properly fitted and oiled trap-doors,—and observing perfect silence, bound his forehead with a white band soaked with blood, and covered with hieroglyphics; they then hung a small crucifix round his neck, and a small satchel containing relics, or what did duty for them. Finally, they took off all his clothing, which they cast on a pyre in one corner of the cave, and marked his body with numerous crosses, drawn with blood. At this point, the hierophant with his assistants entered, and, having bound a red cloth round the middle of the candidate's body, the brethren, clothed in blood-stained garments, placed themselves beside him, and drawing their daggers, formed the steel arch over his head. A carpet being then spread on the floor, all knelt down and prayed for about an hour, after which the pyre was secretly set on fire; the further wall of the cave opened, the air resounded with strains, now gay, now lugubrious, and a long procession of spectres, phantoms, angels, and demons defiled past the neophyte like the "supers" in a pantomime. Whilst this farce was going on, the candidate took the following oath:—" In the name of Christ crucified, I swear to burst the bonds that yet unite me to father, mother, brothers, sisters, relations, friends; to the king, magistrates, and any other authority, to which I may ever have sworn fealty, obedience, gratitude, or service. I renounce .... the place of my birth, henceforth to exist in another sphere. I swear to reveal to my new superior, whom I desire to know, what I have done, thought, read, learnt, or discovered, and to observe and watch all that comes under my notice. I swear to yield myself up to my superior, as if I were a corpse, deprived of life and will. I finally swear to flee temptation, and to reveal all I succeed in discovering, well aware that lightning is not more rapid and ready

than the dagger to reach me wherever I may be."
The new member having taken this oath, was then
introduced into a neighbouring cell, where he took
a bath, and was clothed in garments of new and
white linen. He finally repaired with the other
brethren to a banquet, where he could with choice
food and wine compensate himself for his long ab-
stinence, and the horrors and fatigues he had passed
through.

471. *Blessing the Dagger.*—Blessing the dagger
was a ceremony performed when the society thought
it necessary for their interests to assassinate some
king, prince, or other important personage. By
the side of the Dark Chamber there usually was a
small cell, called the " Cell of Meditation." In its
centre arose a small altar, on which was placed a
painting covered with a veil, and surrounded by
torches and lamps, all of a scarlet colour. Here
the brother whom the Order wished to prepare for
the deed of blood, received his instructions. On a
table stood a casket, covered with strange hieroglyphics and bearing on its lid the representation
of the Lamb. On its being opened, it was found
to contain a dagger, wrapped up in a linen cloth,
which one of the officers of the society took out and
presented to the hierophant; who, after kissing and
sprinkling it with holy water, handed it to one of
the deacons, who attached it like a cross to a rosary,
and hanging it round the neck of the alumnus,

informed him that he was the Elect of God, and told him what victim to strike. A prayer was then offered up in favour of the success of the enterprise, in the following words:—" And Thou, invincible and terrible God, who didst resolve to inspire our Elect and Thy servant with the project of exterminating N. N., a tyrant and heretic, strengthen him, and render the consecration of our brother perfect by the successful execution of the great Work. Increase, O God, his strength a hundred-fold, so that he may accomplish the noble undertaking, and protect him with the powerful and divine armour of thine Elect and Saints. Pour on his head the daring courage which despises all fear, and fortify his body in danger and in the face of death itself." After this prayer the veil was withdrawn from the picture on the altar, and the elect beheld the portrait of the Dominican James Clement, surrounded by a host of angels, carrying him on their wings to celestial glory. And the deacon placing on the head of the chosen brother a crown symbolic of the celestial crown, added:—" Deign, O Lord of hosts, to bestow a propitious glance on the servant Thou hast chosen as *Thine arm*, and for the execution of the high decrees of Thine eternal justice. Amen." Then there were fresh dissolving views of ghosts, spectres, skeletons, phantoms, angels and demons, and the farce, to be followed by a tragedy, was played out.

472. *Secret Instructions.*—It will suffice to give the headings of the chapters forming the Book of Secret Instructions of the Society of Jesus. The Preface specially warns superiors not to allow it to fall into the hands of strangers, as it might give them a bad opinion of the Order. The Chapters are headed as follows :—I. How the Society is to proceed in founding a new establishment.—II. How the Brethren of the Society may acquire and preserve the friendship of Princes and other distinguished Personages.—III. How the Society is to conduct itself towards those who possess great influence in a state ; and who, though they are not rich, may yet be of service to others.—IV. Hints to Preachers and Confessors of Kings and great personages.—V. What conduct to observe towards the clergy and other religious orders. VI. How to win over rich widows.—VII. How to hold fast widows and dispose of their property.—VIII. How to induce the children of widows to adopt a life of religious seclusion.—IX. Of the increase of College revenues.—X. Of the private rigour of discipline to be observed by the society.—XI. How " Ours" shall conduct themselves towards those that have been dismissed from the society.—XII. Whom to keep and make much of in the society.— XIII. How to select young people for admission into the society, and how to keep them there.— XIV. Of reserved cases, and reasons for dismissing

from the society.—XV. How to behave towards nuns and devout women.—XVI. How to pretend contempt for riches.—XVII. General means for advancing the interests of the society.

The intermeddling of this society in the affairs, political, ecclesiastical, and civil, of many countries, is related in numerous works, and repeatedly produced the suppression and expulsion of the order, though it constantly reappeared with new names. In 1716 the French army was infested with Jesuitical and anti-Jesuitical societies. The Parliament of Paris suppressed them in 1762, and this example was followed by other legislators; but still they are to be found everywhere, and they hold considerable property in this country. A modern writer justly calls them the "Black International."

473. *Jehu, Society of.*—This society was formed in France during the revolution, to avenge its excesses by still greater violence. It was first established at Lyons. It took its name from that king who was consecrated by Elijah to punish the sins of the house of Ahab, and to slay all the priests of Baal. The liberals represented the priests. The people, not understanding this, called the society the "Company of Jesus," a very unsuitable name, since the members spread terror and bloodshed throughout France. It was a realistic faction that, under the cloak of politics, concealed its evil passions, and rendered Lyons, Aix, Marseilles,

Bordeaux, and other cities, the theatres of sanguinary tragedies. The faction, however, which seemed for ever destroyed on Napoleon's accession to the throne, re-appeared after his downfall, taking in 1814 the title of " Knights of Maria Theresa," and by them Bordeaux was betrayed into the hands of the English, and the blood of many honoured citizens shed at Nîmes, Montpellier, and other places.

474. *Know-Nothings.*—This was an anti-foreign and no-popery party, formed in the United States of America, and acting chiefly through secret societies, in order to decide the presidential election. It lasted from 1852 to 1856.

475. *Ku-Klux-Klan.* — A secret organization under this name spread with amazing rapidity over the Southern States of the American Union soon after the close of the war. The white people of the South were alarmed, not so much by the threatened confiscation of their property by the Federal government, as by the smaller but more present dangers of life and property, virtue and honour, arising from the social anarchy around them. The negroes, after the Confederate surrender, were disorderly. Many of them would not settle down to labour on any terms, but roamed about with arms in their hands and hunger in their bellies, whilst the governing power was only thinking of every device of suffrage and reconstruction by which the freedmen might be strength-

ened, and made, under Northern dictation, the ruling power in the country. Agitators came down among the towns and plantations; and, organizing a Union league, held midnight meetings with the negroes in the woods, and went about uttering sentiments which were anti-social and destructive. Crimes and outrages increased; the law was all but powerless, and the new governments in the South, supposing them to have been most willing, were certainly unable to repress disorder. A real terror reigned for a time among the white people; and under these circumstances the Ku-Klux started into existence, and executed the Lynch-law, which alone seems effective in disordered states of society. The members wore a dress made of black calico, and called a " shroud." The stuff was sent round to private houses, with a request that it should be made into a garment; and fair fingers sewed it up, and had it ready for the secret messenger when he returned and gave his pre-concerted tap at the door. The women and young girls had faith in the honour of the " Klan," and on its will and ability to protect them. The Ku-Klux, when out on their missions, also wore a high tapering hat, with a black veil over the face. The secret of the membership was kept with remarkable fidelity; and in no instance, it is said, has a member of the Ku-Klux been successfully arraigned and punished, though the Federal government passed a special Act against the society, and two proclamations were issued under this Act by President Grant, as late as October, 1871, and the *habeas corpus* Act suspended in nine counties of South Carolina. When the members had a long ride at night, they made requisitions at farm-houses for horses, which were generally returned on a night following without injury. If a company of Federal soldiers, stationed in a small town, talked loudly as to what they would do with the Ku-Klux, the men in shrouds paraded in the evening before the guard-house in numbers so overwhelming as at once re-duced the little garrison to silence. The overt acts of the Ku-Klux consisted for the most part in dis-arming dangerous negroes, inflicting Lynch-law on notorious offenders, and above all in creating one feeling of terror as a counterpoise to another. The thefts of the negroes were a subject of prevailing complaint in many parts of the South. A band of men in the Ku-Klux costume one night came to the door of Allan Creich, a grocer of Williamson's Creek, seized and dragged him some distance, when they despatched and threw him into the Creek, where his body was found. The assassins then proceeded to the house of Allan's brother, but not finding him at home, they elicited from his little child where he was staying. Hereupon they imme-diately proceeded to the house named ; and, having encountered the man they sought, they dealt with him as they had dealt with his brother Allan. It

appears that Allan had long been blamed for buying
goods and produce stolen by the negroes, and had
often been warned to desist, but without avail. The
institution, like all of a similar nature, though the
necessity for its existence has ceased to a great extent, yet survives in a more degenerate form, having
passed into the hands of utter scoundrels, with no
good motive, and with foul passions of revenge or
plunder, or lust of dread and mysterious power
alone in their hearts. Hence the recent proclamations against it.

476. *Liberty, Knights of.*—A sect formed in
1820 in France against the Government of the
Bourbons. Its independent existence was brief, as
it was soon merged in that of the Carbonari.

477. *Lion, Knights of the.*—This was one of the
transformations assumed in Germany in the last
century by Masonic Templars.

478. *Lion, The Sleeping.*—This was a society
formed in Paris in 1816, with the object of restor-
ing Napoleon to the throne of France. The existing
government suppressed it.

479. *Magi, Order of the.*—Is supposed to have
existed in Italy in the last century, as a modification of the Rosicrucians. Its members are said
to have worn the costume of Inquisitors.

480. *Mahárájas.*— This is an Indian sect of
priests. It appears abundantly from the works of
recognized authority written by Mahárájas, and from

existing popular belief in the Vallabhacharya sect, that Vallabhacharya is believed to have been an incarnation of the god Krishna, and that the Mahárájas, as descendants of Vallabhacharya, have claimed and received from their followers the like character of incarnations of that god by hereditary succession. The ceremonies of the worship paid to Krishna through these priests are all of the most licentious character. The love and subserviency due to a Supreme Being are here materialized and transferred to those who claim to be the living incarnations of the god. Hence the priests exercise an unlimited influence over their female votaries, who consider it a great honour to acquire the temporary regard of the voluptuous Mahárájas, the belief in whose pretensions is allowed to interfere, almost vitally, with the domestic relations of husband and wife. The Mahárája libel case, tried in 1862 in the Supreme Court of Bombay, proved that the wealthiest and largest of the Hindoo mercantile communities of Central and Western India worshipped as a god a depraved priest, compared with whom an ancient satyr was an angel. Indeed, on becoming followers of that god, they make to his priest the offering of *tan, man,* and *dhan,* or body, mind, and property; and so far does their folly extend that they will greedily drink the water in which he has bathed. There are about seventy or eighty of the Mahárájas in different parts of India. They have a mark on the forehead, consisting of two red perpendicular lines, meeting in a semi-circle at the root of the nose, and having a round spot of red between them. Though not a secret society, strictly speaking, still, as its doings were to some extent kept secret, and their worst features, though proved by legal evidence, denied by the persons implicated, I have thought it right to give it a place here.

481. *Nemesis.*—A society formed in 1842 at Paris, which, the better to intimate its intentions, also called itself the "Revolutionary Tribunal, One and Indivisible." When discovered by government, it counted twenty-two members.

482. *O-Kee-Pa.*—A religious rite, commemorative of the flood, which was practised by the Mandans, a now extinct tribe of Red Indians. The celebration was annual, and its object threefold, viz. :—(1) to keep in remembrance the subsiding of the waters ; (2) to dance the bull-dance, to insure a plentiful supply of buffaloes (though the reader will see in it an allusion to the bull of the zodiac, the vernal equinox); and (3) to test the courage and power of endurance of the young men who, during the past year, had arrived at the age of manhood, by great bodily privations and tortures. Part of the latter were inflicted in the secresy of the "Medicine-hut," outside of which stood the Big Canoe, or Mandan Ark, which only the "Mystery-Men" were allowed to touch or look into. The

tortures, as witnessed by Catlin, consisted in forcing sticks of wood under the dorsal or pectoral muscles of the victim, and then suspending him by these sticks from the top of the hut, and turning him round until he fainted, when he was taken down and allowed to recover consciousness ; whereupon he was driven forth among the multitude assembled without, who chased him round the village, treading on the cords attached to the bits of wood sticking in his flesh, until these latter fell out by tearing the flesh to pieces. Like the ancient mysteries, the O-Kee-Pa ended with drunken and vicious orgies.

483. *Pantheists.*—A German society in which the maxims contained in Toland's " Pantheisticon" were discussed.

484. *Phi-Beta-Kappa.*—The Bavarian Illuminati, according to some accounts, spread to America, where they adopted the above grotesque title.

485. *Pilgrims.*—A society, whose existence was discovered at Lyons in 1825, through the arrest of one of the brethren, a Prussian shoemaker, on whom was found the printed catechism of the society. Though the Pilgrims aimed above all at religious reform, yet their catechism was modelled on that of the Freemasons.

486. *The Purrah.*—Between the river of Sierra Leone and Cape Monte, there exist five nations of Foulahs-Sousous, who form among themselves a

kind of federative republic. Each colony has its particular magistrates and local government; but they are subject to an institution which they call *Purrah.* It is an association of warriors, which from its effects is very similar to the secret tribunal formerly existing in Germany and known by the name of the Holy Vehm (166) ; and on account of its rites and mysteries closely resembles the ancient initiations. Each of the five colonies has its own peculiar Purrah, consisting of twenty-five members; and from each of these particular tribunals are taken five persons, who form the Grand Purrah or supreme tribunal.

To be admitted to a district Purrah the candidate must be at least thirty years of age; to be a member of the Grand Purrah, he must be fifty years old. All his relations belonging to the Purrah become security for the candidate's conduct, and bind themselves by oath to sacrifice him, if he flinch during the ceremony, or if, after having been admitted, he betray the mysteries and tenets of the association.

In each district comprised in the institution of the Purrah there is a sacred wood whither the candidate is conducted, and where he is confined for several months in a solitary and contracted habitation, and neither speaks nor quits the dwelling assigned to him. If he attempt to penetrate into the forest which surrounds him, he is instantly slain. After several months' preparation the candidate is admitted to the trial, the last proofs of which are said to be terrible. All the elements are employed to ascertain his resolution and courage; lions and leopards, in some degree chained, are made use of; during the time of the proof the sacred woods resound with dreadful howlings; conflagrations appear in the night, seeming to indicate general destruction; while at other times fire is seen to pervade these mysterious woods in all directions. Every one whose curiosity excites him to profane these sacred parts, is sacrificed without mercy. When the candidate has undergone all the degrees of probation, he is permitted to be initiated, an oath being previously exacted from him that he will keep all the secrets, and execute without demur all the decrees of the Purrah of his tribe or of the Grand and Sovereign Purrah.

Any member turning traitor or rebel is devoted to death, and sometimes assassinated in the midst of his family. At a moment when a guilty person least expects it, a warrior appears before him, masked and armed, who says:—"The Sovereign Purrah decrees thy death." On these words every person present shrinks back, no one makes the least resistance, and the victim is killed. The common Purrah of a tribe takes cognizance of the crimes committed within its jurisdiction, tries the criminals, and executes their sentences; and also appeases the quarrels that arise among powerful families.

It is only on extraordinary occasions that the Grand Purrah assembles for the trial of those who betray the mysteries and secrets of the order, or rebel against its dictates; and it is this assembly which generally puts an end to the wars that sometimes break out between two or more tribes. From the moment when the Grand Purrah has assembled for the purpose of terminating a war, till it has decided on the subject, every warrior of the belligerent parties is forbidden to shed a drop of blood under pain of death. The deliberations of the Purrah generally last a month, after which the guilty tribe is condemned to be pillaged during four days. The warriors who execute the sentence are taken from the neutral cantons; and they disguise themselves with frightful masks, are armed with poniards, and carry lighted torches. They arrive at the doomed villages before break of day, kill all the inhabitants that cannot make their escape, and carry off whatever property of value they can find. The plunder is divided into two parts; one part being allotted to the tribe against which the aggression had been committed, whilst the other part goes to the Grand Purrah, which distributes it among the warriors who executed the sentence.

When any family of the tribes under the command of the Purrah becomes too powerful and excites alarm, the Grand Purrah assembles to deliberate on the subject, and almost always condemns it to sudden and unexpected pillage; which is executed by night, and always by warriors masked and disguised.

The terror and alarm which this confederation excites amongst the inhabitants of the countries where it is established, and even in the neighbouring territories, are very great. The negroes of the Bay of Sierra Leone never speak of it without reserve and apprehension; for they believe that all the members of the confederation are sorcerers, and that they have communication with the devil. The Purrah has an interest in propagating these prejudices, by means of which it exercises an authority that no person dares to dispute. The number of members is supposed to be about 6,000, and they recognize each other by certain words and signs.

487. *The Rebeccaites.—The Hunters.*—The first was a society formed in Wales, for the abolition of toll-bars. Like the Irish Whiteboys, the members dressed in white, and went about at night pulling down the toll-gates. Government suppressed them. In 1837, after the first Canadian insurrection, a society of malcontents was formed under the title of " Hunters," whose object was to bring about a second insurrection. But the society lasted only for two years, and ended in smoke.

488. *Redemption, Order of.*—A secret and chivalrous society, which in its organization copied the order of the Knights of Malta. Its scope is

scarcely known, and it never went beyond the walls of Marseilles, where it was founded by a Sicilian exile.

489. *Regeneration, Society of Universal.*—It was composed of the patriots of various countries, who had taken refuge in Switzerland between 1815 and 1820. But though their aims were very comprehensive, they ended in talk, of which professed patriots always have a liberal supply on hand.

490. *Sikh Fanatics.*—The new phase of Sikh fanaticism, which recently revealed its existence by the Kooka murders, may be traced to the following sources:—The movement was started a good many years since by one Ram Singh, a Sikh, whose headquarters were fixed at the village of Bainee in the Loodhiana district. His teaching is said to have aimed at reforming the ritual rather than the creed of his countrymen. His followers, moreover, seem to have borrowed a hint or two from the dancing dervishes of Islam. At their meetings they worked themselves into a sort of religious frenzy, which relieved itself by unearthly howlings, and hence they were generally known as the "Shouters." Men and women of the new sect joined together in a sort of wild war-dance, yelling out certain forms of words, and stripping off all their clothing, as they whirled more and more rapidly round. Ram Singh himself had served in the old Sikh army, and one of his first moves was to get a number of his emissaries enlisted

into the army of the Maharajah of Cashmere. That ruler, it is said, would have taken a whole regiment of Kookas into his pay; but for some reason or another this scheme fell to the ground. Possibly he took fright at the political influence which his new recruits might come in time to wield against him or his English allies. Ram Singh's followers, however, multiplied apace; and out of their number he chose his lieutenants, whose preaching in time swelled the total of converts to something like 100,000. Of these *soubahs*, or lieutenants, some twenty were distributed about the Punjaub. The great bulk of their converts consisted of artisans and people of yet lower caste, who, having nothing to lose, indulged in wild dreams of future gain. Their leader's power over them appears to have been very great. They obeyed his orders as cheerfully as the Assassins of yore obeyed the Old Man of the Mountain. If he had a message to send to one of his lieutenants, however far away, a letter was intrusted to one of his disciples, who ran full speed to the next station, and handed it to another, who forthwith left his own work, and hastened in like manner to deliver the letter to a third. In order to clinch his power over his followers, Ram Singh contrived to interpolate his own name in a passage of the " Grunth "—the Sikh Bible—which foretels the advent of another *Guru*, prophet or teacher. But, whatever the teachings of this new religious leader, there is reason to think that his ultimate aim was to restore the Sikhs to their old supremacy in the Punjaub by means of a religious revival. Secret murder and savage intimidation appear to have been the weapons most frequently used to that end. Ram Singh's name was connected with a brutal murder which happened in 1868; and his complicity with the recent outrages of Umritsur and Raekote seems to have been placed beyond question by the appeal which one of his disciples made to him in open court. On his denial of the charge, his deluded follower replied, that he had always been taught to tell the truth, and now his own teacher lied. For the present, at any rate, a heavy blow appears to have been dealt at this movement by the promptitude with which punishment followed crime. No new disciples are coming forward, and many are said to be falling away. Still a body nearly 100,000 strong, bound together by a common fanaticism, and impatient of foreign rule, will need very careful watching on our part.

491. *Tobaccological Society.*—One of the most bizarre of Masonic variations with four degrees, that professed to teach the doctrines of Pythagoras, and which arose during the middle of the last century. The tobacco plant, its culture and manufacture, were the subjects of symbolical instructions, the catechisms of which are still extant.

492. *Universalists.*—A Masonic society of one degree, established at Paris in 1841.

493. *Thirteen, The.*—A society that exercised an occult influence in Paris during the First Empire. Balzac has founded on it one of his most charming romances.

494. *Thugs.*—This association, after having existed in India for centuries, was only discovered in 1810. The names by which the members were known to each other, and also to others, was Funsiegeer, that is, "men of the noose." The name Thug is said to be derived from *thaga*, to deceive, because the Thugs get hold of their victims by luring them into false security. One common mode of decoying young men having valuables upon them is to place a young and handsome woman by the wayside, and apparently in great grief, who, by some pretended tale of misfortune, draws him into the jungle, where the gang are lying in ambush, and on his appearance strangle him. The gang consists of from ten to fifty members; and they will follow or accompany the marked-out victim for days, nor attempt his murder until an opportunity, offering every chance of success, presents itself. After every murder they perform a religious ceremony, called *jagmi;* and the division of the spoil is regulated by old-established laws—the man that threw the handkerchief gets the largest share, the man that held the hands the next largest proportion, and so on. In some gangs their property is held in common. Their crimes are committed in honour of

Káli, who hates our race, and to whom the death of man is a pleasing sacrifice.

Káli, or Bhowany, for she is equally well known by both names, was, according to the Indian legend, born of the burning eye which Shiva, one of the persons of the Brahmin trinity, has on his forehead, whence she issued, like the Greek Minerva out of the skull of Jupiter, a perfect and full-grown being. She represents the Evil Spirit, delights in human blood, presides over plague and pestilence, and directs the storm and hurricane, and ever aims at destruction. She is represented under the most frightful effigy the Indian mind could conceive; her face is azure, streaked with yellow; her glance is ferocious; she wears her dishevelled and bristly hair displayed like the peacock's tail and braided with green serpents. Her purple lips seem streaming with blood; her tusk-like teeth descend over her lower lip; she has eight or ten arms, each hand holding some murderous weapon, and sometimes a human head dripping with gore. With one foot she stands on a human corpse. She has her temples, in which the people sacrifice cocks and bullocks to her; but her priests are the Thugs, the " Sons of Death," who quench the never-ending thirst of this divine vampyre.

495. *Traditions.*—Like all similar societies, the Thugs have their traditions. According to them, Káli in the beginning determined to destroy the

whole human race, with the exception, however, of her faithful adorers and followers. These, taught by her, slew all men that fell into their power. The victims at first were killed by the sword, and so great was the destruction her worshippers wrought, that the whole human race would have been extinguished, had not Vishnu, the Preserver, interfered, by causing the blood thus shed to bring forth new living beings, so that the destructive action of Káli was counteracted. It was then this goddess, to nullify the good intention of Vishnu, forbade her followers to kill any more with the sword, but commanded them to resort to strangulation. With her own hands she made a human figure of clay, and animated it with her breath. She then taught her worshippers how to kill without shedding blood. She also promised them that she would always bury the bodies of their victims, and destroy all traces of them. She further endowed her chosen disciples with superior courage and cunning, so as always to ensure them the victory over those they should attack. And she kept her promise. But in the course of time corrupt manners crept in even among the Thugs, and one of them, being curious to see what Káli did with the dead bodies, watched her, as she was about to remove the corpse of a traveller he had slain. Goddesses, however, cannot thus be watched on the sly. Bhowany saw the peeper, and stepping forth, thus addressed him :—

" Thou hast now beheld the awful countenance of a goddess, which none can behold and live. But I shall spare thy days, though as a punishment of thy crime, I shall not protect thee as I have done hitherto, and the punishment will extend to all thy brethren. The corpses of those you kill will no longer be buried or concealed by me; you yourselves will be obliged to take the necessary measures for that purpose, nor will you always be successful; sometimes you will fall under the profane laws of the world, which will be your eternal punishment. Nothing will remain to you but the superior intelligence and skill I have given you, and henceforth I shall direct you by auguries only, which you must diligently consult." Hence their superstitious belief in omens. They study divination by birds and jackals, and by throwing the hatchet, and as it falls so they take their route. Any animal crossing the road from left to right, on their first setting out, is considered a bad omen, and the expedition consequently is given up for that day.

Strange that in the corrupted traditions of Thugs, murderers and thieves, we should encounter first the ancient idea of the spontaneous birth of knowledge, both of good and evil; further, the prototype of the beautiful fable of Cupid and Psyche, and the Mosaic account of the fall of man; and thirdly, the enunciation of the impossibility of

II.   Y

comprehending—for " seeing " here has this meaning—the Universal Intelligence.

496. *Initiation.*—To be admitted into this horrible
sect required a long and severe novitiate, during
which the aspirant had to give the most convincing
proofs of his fitness for admission. This having
once been decided on, he was conducted by his
sponsor to the mystical baptism, and clothed in
white garments and his brow crowned with flowers.
The preparatory rite being performed, the sponsor
presented him to the gurhù, or spiritual head of the
sect, who, in his turn, introduced him into a room
set apart for such ceremonies, where the Hye-
mader, or chiefs of the various gangs, awaited him.
Being asked whether they will receive the candidate
into the order, and having answered in the affirma-
tive, he and the gurhù are led out into the open
air, where the chiefs place themselves in a circle
around the two, and kneel down to pray. Then
the gurhù rises, and lifting up his hands to heaven,
says :—" O Bhowany ! Mother of the world ! " (this
appellation seems very inappropriate, since she is a
destroyer,) " whose worshippers we are, receive this
Thy new servant; grant him Thy protection, and
to us an omen, which assures us of Thy consent."
They remain in this position, until a passing bird,
quadruped, or even mere cloud, has given them
this assurance ; whereupon they return to the
chamber, where the neophyte is invited to partake

of a banquet spread out for the occasion, after which the ceremony is over. The newly admitted member then takes the appellation of *Sahib-Zada*. He commences his infamous career as *lughah*, or grave-digger, or as *belhal*, or explorer of the spots most convenient for executing a projected assassination, or *bhil*. In this condition he remains for several years, until he has given abundant proof of his ability and good will. He is then raised to the degree of *bhuttotah*, or strangler, which advancement, however, is preceded by new formalities and ceremonies. On the day appointed for the ceremony, the candidate is conducted by his gurhù into a circle, formed in the sands and surrounded by mysterious hieroglyphics, where prayers are offered up to their deity. The ceremony lasts four days, during which the candidate is allowed no other food but milk. He occupies himself in practising the immolation of victims fastened to a cross erected in the ground. On the fifth day the priest gives him the fatal noose, washed in holy water and anointed with oil, and after more religious ceremonies, he is pronounced a perfect bhuttotah. He binds himself by fearful oaths to maintain the most perfect silence on all that concerns the society, and to labour without ceasing towards the destruction of the human race. He is the *rex sacrificulus*, and the person he encounters, and Bhowany places in his way, the victim. Certain

persons, however, are excepted from the attacks of
the Thugs. The hierophant, on initiating the
candidate, says to him:—" Thou hast chosen, my
son, the most ancient profession, the most accept-
able to the deity. Thou hast sworn to put to death
every human being fate throws into thy hand;
there are, however, some that are exempt from our
laws, and whose death would not be grateful to our
deity." These belong to some particular tribes
and castes, which he enumerates; persons who
squint, are lame, or otherwise deformed, are also
exempt; so are washerwomen, for some cause not
clearly ascertained; and as Káli was supposed to co-
operate with the murderers, women also were safe
from them, but only when travelling alone, without
male protector; and orthodox Thugs date the de-
terioration of Thuggism from the first murder of a
woman by some members of the society, after
which the practice became common.

The Thugs had their saints and martyrs, Thora
and Kudull being two of the most famous, who are
invoked by the followers of Bhowany. Worshippers
of a deity delighting in blood, those whom the
English Government condemned to death, offered
her their own lives with the same readiness with
which they had taken those of others. They met
death with indifference, nay, with enthusiasm,
firmly believing that they should at once enter
paradise. The only favour they asked, was to be

strangled or hanged; they have an intense horror of the sword and the shedding of blood, as they killed by the cord, so they wished to die by it.

497. *Suppression.*—When the existence of the society was first discovered, many would not believe in it; yet in course of time the proofs became so convincing that it could no longer be ignored, and the British Government took decided measures to suppress the Thugs. The crimes some of them had committed, indeed, almost exceed belief. One Thug, who was hanged at Lucknow in 1825, was legally convicted of having strangled six hundred persons. Another, an octogenarian, confessed to nine hundred and ninety-nine murders, and declared that respect for the profession alone had prevented him from making it a full thousand, because a round number was considered among them rather vulgar. But in spite of vigorous measures on the part of Great Britain, the sect could not be entirely destroyed; it is a religious order, and as such has a vitality greater than that of political or merely criminal associations. It was still in existence but a few years ago, and no doubt has its adherents even now. It always had protectors in some of the native princes, who shared their booty, and such may now be the case. The society has a temple at Mirzapore, on the Ganges.

A Thug, who during the Indian rebellion turned informer, confessed to having strangled three women, besides, perhaps, one hundred men. Yet this fellow was most pleasing and amiable in appearance and manners; but, when relating his deeds of blood, he would speak of them with all the enthusiasm of an old warrior remembering heroic feats, and all the instincts of the tiger seemed to re-awaken in him. In spite of this, however, he caused some two hundred of his old companions to be apprehended by our government.

498. *Wahabees.*—This sect, the members of which lately attracted considerable attention on account of their suspected connection with the murder of Chief Justice Norman at Calcutta, has the following origin :—About 1740, a Mahommedan reformer appeared in Nejd, named Abdu'l Waháb, and conquered great part of Arabia from the Turks. He died in 1787, having founded a sect known as the Wahábees, who took Mecca and Medina, and almost expelled the Turk from the Land of the Prophet. But in 1818, the power of these fierce reformers waned in Arabia, only to re-appear in India, under a new leader, one Saiyid Ahmad, who had been a godless trooper in the plundering bands of Amir Khan, the first Nawab of Tonk. But in 1816 he went to Delhi to study law, and his fervid imagination drank in greedily the new subject. He became absorbed in meditation, which degenerated into epileptic trances, in which he saw visions. In three years he left Delhi as a new prophet; and, journeying to Patna and Cal-

cutta, was surrounded by admiring crowds, who hung upon his accents, and received with ecstasy the divine lesson to slay the infidel, and drive the armies of the foreigner from India. In 1823, he passed through Bombay to Rohilkhand, and having there raised an army of the faithful, he crossed the land of the Five Rivers, and settled like a thunder-cloud on the mountains to the north-east of Peshawur. Since then the rebel camp thus founded has been fed from the head centre at Patna with bands of fanatics and money raised by taxing the faithful. Twenty sanguinary campaigns against this rebel host, aided by the surrounding Afghan tribes, have failed to dislodge them; and they remain to encourage any invader of India, any enemy of the English, to whom they would undoubtedly afford immense assistance ("Athenæum," 26th Aug. 1871). Though the general impression in England and India seems to be that the murder of Mr. Norman is not to be attributed to a Wahábee plot; yet so little is known of the constitution, numerical strength, and aims of the secret societies of India, that an overweening confidence in the loyalty of the *alien* masses—as the "Times" curiously enough terms them, I suppose in imitation of Mrs. Ramsbottom, who was so very indignant, when living in France, at being called a *foreigner*—on the part of the English residents in India, is greatly to be condemned. "This dreadful murder," says the "Telegraph," "is a rea-

son for intelligent and unremitting vigilance among
the chiefs of the police, for public and unyielding
defiance of danger among all our English officials,
and for sharp watchfulness by the Government of
that nest of Wahábee fanatics on the northern frontiers."

499. *Yellow Caps, Society of the.*—A society
said to have been founded in China, under the reign
of Sing-Ti, in the second century of our era, num-
bering among its members the flower of Chinese
littérateurs, who aimed at political power.

THE END.

ABOUT THE AUTHOR

Charles William Heckethorn was born in Switzerland, around 1826. His early years appear to have been spent in Basel but he later moved to Britain and became a naturalised British citizen. In 1850 he was "Professor of French and German in Mr. Bass's School Ryde, Isle of Wight". He married Sarah Forsyth in 1851. When his wife Sarah died, in 1895, he married Jane Baker and they had a daughter, Wilhelmine J. Heckethorn (born around 1879).

Heckethorn's first book was *Exercises in French orthography*, published in 1850 while he was working at Mr. Bass's School Ryde, Isle of Wight. He then produced a translation of *The Frithjof Saga by Esaias Tegnér* in 1856. He did not produce another book until 1875 (foreword dated 1874) when his two volume history, *The secret societies of all ages and countries*, was published. A second edition was published in 1897 and a German language edition in 1900.

In 1875, Heckethorn produced *Roba d'Italia, or, Italian lights and shadows*, an account of a journey through Italy, which was criticised by *The Literary Review* for plagiarising *Roba di Roma*. The journal then alternately criticised and praised the book for its eccentric nature and digressions before heartily recommending it to its readers. The papal anecdotes were found to be amusing but a strong antithesis to the church was noted throughout the work that condemned the waste of teaching the dimensions of Solomon's temple while the *"laws of nature and scientific truths"* were neglected.

Heckethorn then produced books at regular intervals including poetry and children's stories, and a history of the Lincoln's Inn Fields area. His last work, *London memories*, was published in 1900 and contained a chapter on the history of South Lambeth Road. The book was criticised in *The Spectator* for its arrogant view of the past which condemned earlier generations as *"barbarians in manners, and in morals reprobates"* and contained the claim that *"nothing will elevate man but science"*.

Heckethorn died on 13 January 1902 at his home in South Lambeth Road, London.

Selected publications

- *Exercises in French orthography, on a plan entirely new &c.* Relfe & Fletcher, London, 1850.
- *The Frithjof Saga ... Translated into English in the original metres.* Trübner & Co., London, 1856.
- *The secret societies of all ages and countries.* Richard Bentley, London, 1875 (2 vols.)

- *Roba d'Italia, or, Italian lights and shadows: A record of travel.* Samuel Tinsley, London, 1875.
- *Roses and thorns: Poems.* B. Dobell, London, 1888.
- *The windmill and its secrets. A Dove Dale romance.* Trübner & Co., London, 1888.
- *The wondrous tale of Cocky, Clucky, and Cackle. Freely translated from the German of Brentano by C.W. Heckethorn.* J. Hogg, London, 1889.
- *Lincoln's Inn Fields and the localities adjacent: Their historical and topographical associations.* Elliott Stock. London, 1896.
- *The printers of Basle in the XV & XVI centuries: Their biographies, printed books and devices.* Unwin, London, 1897.
- *London souvenirs.* Chatto & Windus, London, 1899.
- *London memories, social, historical, and topographical.* Chatto and Windus, London, 1900.